Walk!
La Palma

with

Charles Davis

DISCOVERY WALKING GUIDES LTD

Walk! La Palma
First Edition - March 2005

Copyright © 2005

Published by
Discovery Walking Guides Ltd
10 Tennyson Close, Northampton NN5 7HJ,
England

Maps
Maps are adapted from **La Palma Tour & Trail
Map** (ISBN 1-904946-07-0) published by
Discovery Walking Guides Ltd

Photographs
Photographs on pages 42, 46, 48, 50, 51, 54, 57, 60,
61, 64, 71, 97, 106, 111, 112 and 116 were taken by
the author, Charles Davis, and Jeanette Tallegas.
All other photographs were taken by David & Ros
Brawn

Front Cover Photographs

Walk 7 Approaching
the summit from the
south

Walk 34, the narrow stretch
on the ridge

Walk 10, ascending Teneguia

On Walk 27, The
Devil's Wall

ISBN 1-904946-06-2
Text and photographs* © Charles Davis

Walk! La Palma

CONTENTS

THE WALKS

SOUTH: SANTA CRUZ DE LA PALMA to TAZACORTE

NORTH-EAST: EL TABLADO to SANTA CRUZ DE LA PALMA

CALDERA DE TABURIENTE

Charles Davis was born in London, and has lived and worked in the United States, Sudan, Turkey, Ivory Coast, Spain and France. With the onset of middle age, he realised that the urge to roam was better satisfied by walking than bouncing about on the back of a lorry in the middle of the desert, and now divides his time between mountain tops, desk-tops and laptops. He is the author of numerous highly praised and wholly unpublished novels.

Jeanette Tallegas has spent thirty odd years labouring for the French education system, from which she has finally, gleefully, taken early retirement. Asked what she intends doing now, she resolutely replies, "Nothing". Nonetheless, she does follow the author up various gruelling mountains, frequently alarming younger walkers who seem to assume that remote and inaccessible places are the preserve of youth.

Bati, (an Old English Sheepdog) is sadly is no longer with us. However, he was sufficiently winsome to overcome the author's prejudice against pedigree dogs, and was consequently plucked from the Municipal Dog Pound where he had been dumped by his previous owners. Despite initial misgivings (he expressed a strong preference for staying in the car), he became quite mad about mountains.

Charles Davis is also the author of:-

34 Alpujarras Walks ISBN 1-899554-83-1

Walk! La Gomera (2nd Edition) ISBN 1-899554-90-4

Walk! Mallorca (North & Mountains) ISBN 1-899554-92-0

Walk! Mallorca West ISBN 1-899554-98-X

Walk! Axarquía ISBN 1-904946-08-9

Walk! Andorra ISBN 1-904946-04-6

- published by Discovery Walking Guides Ltd.

The steepest island in the world, the deepest crater, the clearest skies; volcanoes you can climb without being shot into orbit; a subtropical forest minus the slimy things slinking up your trouser leg; black beaches, blue seas, high mountains, vegetation that is literally flamboyant, everything linked by 1080 kilometres of waymarked paths; and all virtually untouched by tourism. If this sounds divine or like some lost paradise, you're not the first to think so, previous commentators having identified La Palma as the prototype for both the Elysian Fields and Atlantis! The fanciful stuff aside, the island is a walker's idyll, utterly tranquil, verdant, and almost entirely unspoiled.

THE ISLAND

The Green Island or, more commonly, The Beautiful Island, La Palma is essentially a large question mark with a lot of rock draped around it. The question mark is formed by a central spine of volcanic mountains, the **Cumbre Vieja**, linked by the **Cumbre Nueva** to the loop of the **Caldera de Taburiente**, the largest water erosion crater in the world.

The north is wild and green, mantled in a blanket of dense forest thanks to the humidity brought by the trade winds, and so scoured with ravines the first metalled road was only laid in the last decade and there wasn't even a dirt track till the late fifties.

The south is a frazzled wasteland, blackened by volcanoes and thinly forested, relying largely on banana plantations and pockets of malmsey viniculture to give it a thin green fringe. Thirty-five percent of the island is officially protected, but the three most celebrated areas are the volcanoes of the **Cumbre Vieja**, the **Caldera** (literally 'cauldron') de **Taburiente**, and the **Los Tilos** World Biosphere Reserve forest.

Steepness is perhaps the defining quality of La Palma. Relative to landmass, it's the steepest island in the world and, seen from the **Cumbre Vieja** at sunset, the island's shadow reaches all the way to Tenerife, 85km away! This steepness, along with a lack of golden sands and money (apart from bananas, La Palma's principle export has been people, largely to South America, which has had a corresponding impact on local culture, cuisine and agriculture), have saved the island from mass tourism to such an extent that old black and white photos on bar walls, elsewhere an eloquent testimony to tiny fishing hamlets transformed into dense tower hamlets, might in La Palma have been taken yesterday for all that's changed.

AIM & SCOPE

This book is aimed at the independent traveller who either wishes to structure a trip round daily walks or break up a conventional holiday with the occasional walk. Our brief was to outline a network of 2-4 hour routes using the new system of waymarked paths. There are walks to suit all tastes and capacities, covering all the classic itineraries, in whole or in part, plus several obscure but no less attractive 'new' routes.

The climate is essentially subtropical but is relieved of oppressive heat by the trade winds. Statistics suggest a very moderate year-round change in temperature, but this doesn't reflect the dramatic changes to be experienced according to shifts in altitude and cloud cover. On the north-eastern side of the island there is an almost permanent band of cloud, hovering around 1000 metres in summer and 500 metres in winter.

Our research was done in July and August, so the walks are possible in hot weather, though it's best to finish by midday. Most walkers come in winter, a preference reflected in the availability of direct flights, but bear in mind that temperatures at the highest point of the island can drop to zero at this time of year. Regardless of temperature, cover up in high places, where the sun is always intense.

GETTING THERE, GETTING ABOUT, GETTING A BED

Santa Cruz de La Palma port

JMC have weekly **flights** in winter, otherwise there's a daily Fred Olsen **ferry** from Tenerife, and a weekly Trasmediterranea ferry from Cádiz, calling at Gran Canaria and Tenerife en route.

Hire-car is the simplest way of getting about. There are several agencies at the airport and every second shop in **Santa Cruz**, the capital and ferry-port, seems to offer its own rental service.

Twenty routes are accessible by **bus**, though the service on some lines is limited (especially at weekends) and certain roads are so windy you might not feel like walking after being swirled about in a bus. Where appropriate, bus times are mentioned in walk descriptions, but call at the Tourist Office for up-to-date information. Also see Bus Timetables on Pages 135-137.

Hitching might be practical in the north where several walks start well off the bus route. There isn't much traffic, but I can't imagine anyone would be so mean as to pass a hitchhiker on such tiny country lanes.

Taxi drivers are used to dropping people off and (hopefully) picking them up again at the start and finish of more popular routes, though this is a comparatively expensive option. In the preliminary notes for each itinerary, **TF** = 'taxi-friendly' i.e. car-access walks feasible and affordable by taxi; **TF$**

= feasible but expensive (€30+); **4X4T** = feasible but probably only accepted by 4X4 taxis. See Appendices for taxi phone numbers.

Outside **Santa Cruz** and the few small beach resorts, single room **accommodation** is scarce, but there's a good spread of *Casas Rurales* available for weekly rental. See the Appendices.

There is a fully-equipped **campsite** at **Laguna de Barlovento**, partially equipped camping areas at **San Antonio**, inside the **Caldera** (1 night only) and at **El Pilar** (up to 7 nights), the last two requiring a permit, free on request from the **El Paso Centro de Visitantes**; **Fuencaliente** football pitch also doubles as a camping area. Contact details are in the Appendices.

WHAT'S IN A NAME?

One surprising aspect of La Palma is that nobody can decide what to call anything, a general principal that applies to roads, buses, towns, and natural features. **Road numbers** are a mystery, boasting so many aliases one begins to wonder whether they're not going incognito. Junctions, kilometre markings, and (other publishers'!) maps all have their own idea as to what should be what. This isn't terribly helpful when you're trying to get your bearings, but it's part of the charm of La Palma that nobody much fussed what a road's called so long as it gets you where you're going – eventually. When I refer to a road in the text I will give the names of the places it links to avoid confusion.

On our map, we have followed the official local government numbering (different from the national government numbering, some of which appears on recent maps but nowhere on the ground!) on the assumption that they are the people most likely to do something about making the junction and kilometre markers coherent. On the ground, if in doubt, ask for the *Carretera General*: this will usually elicit directions to the main road. The confusion of road numbers is echoed by the numbers on front of **buses**, which don't correspond to the published <u>line</u> number.

Also bear in mind that many **towns** have two names, for example **Breña Alta** is **San Pedro**, **Fuencaliente** is **Los Canarios**, and **Garafía** is **Santo Domingo**: this is not some cunning ruse conjured up by the locals to confuse foreigners, but a reflection of discrete village names within a larger administrative district; for example, **Santo Domingo** is the central village of the **Garafía** area.

Barrancos or ravines (even if you don't speak Spanish, this is one word you'll never forget after a visit to La Palma) are also confusing, often boasting three distinct names from top to bottom of the same ravine. It's true, they are very big, but three names can seem excessive. That said, the profligacy of naming seems to have caught up with the original settlers who, Noah-like, have elected to have **two of everything**. Bear this in mind if you see a **Barranco del Agua** or **de los Gomeros**, a **Las Tricias**, or a **Volcán San Juan** signposted somewhere it ought not to be.

A lot of time, thought and energy have been invested in waymarking a bewildering selection of paths on La Palma: two *Gran Recorridos* (GR) or long-distance footpaths, over 40 *Pequeño Recorridos* (PR) or 'short' distance footpaths and almost as many *Senderos Locales* (SL), linking paths or local strolls. However, few paths are practical in their entirety as single day excursions and, if so, are not necessarily desirable, either because they climb to places otherwise accessible by road or descend from places inaccessible by public transport.

I've tried to avoid routes climbing to a point one can reach by road and have aimed for as many **circuits** as possible. It's customary in books about La Palma to include day-long linear routes involving a combination of buses and taxis (not to mention a wing and a prayer) at either end. With two exceptions (Walks 8&25, both very exceptional), I've steered clear of this, as the logistics and timetabling involved take a lot of the pleasure out of the walk, turning walking into a military exercise. 25 walks end and start at the same point, 7 returning by the same route.

There are more **linear walks** than I would have preferred (16), but on the steepest island in the world you either go linear or go barmy, climbing 1000 metres to no particular purpose other than putting the loop into loopy and reaching a road you probably used to get to the start of the walk in the first place. In sum: there are 18 circuits, 9 one-way linear walks (2 involving taxis, the rest on mainline bus routes), and 7 two-way linear walks.

All walks are walks and require no special **expertise**, though another consequence of the island's steepness is that some itineraries are inevitably vertiginous, notably those following canalisation pipes, which can be very dangerous and are only recommended for experienced walkers. Where relevant, I will specify the risk of **vertigo** in the itinerary introduction.

You will occasionally see references to **controlled-skidding** when descending through *picón*, the volcanic grit encountered on many walks in the south. Don't be alarmed by this. It's not a new folly dreamed up by the Dangerous Sports club but the inevitable consequence of steep slopes and deep grit. The trick is to get your heels stuck in and try not to stand on any large rocks. Apart from that, grit and gravity take care of the rest. Pure child's play.

On the whole, **access** is not a problem, though the new *Plan de Autoprotección de la Caldera* does stipulate certain restrictions on access to the interior of the **Caldera**: large groups must have a guide and, on hot and windy days when there's a risk of fire, no more than 100 people can enter the crater.

Within each section, the first walk is suitable as a **test walk** for the first day and the second walk is a slightly more ambitious itinerary for the second day. The remaining walks are arranged in a vaguely geographical order, not according to difficulty or length.

Timings are all 'pure' timings excluding snacking, snapping and simply standing still staring. It's highly unlikely you will complete any of these walks in exactly the time specified. Try one of the shorter walks first to see how your times compare to mine. As a rule of thumb, add fifteen minutes to every timed hour. But above all, take YOUR time. There's nothing more frustrating than trying to walk at somebody else's pace, be it slower or faster than yours. All global timings include the return unless otherwise specified. Given the island's steepness, driving to the top is an ear-battering experience; you may wish to add twenty minutes to walks round the rim of the **Caldera** for acclimatising.

Length: I have aimed at 2-4 hour walks suitable for a half-day outing, though there are several shorter excursions, either discrete itineraries or short versions of longer walks, and a few are necessarily longer. If you're interested in longer treks, these are amply covered by the official waymarked routes, though beware of PRs intended as day-long itineraries – most of them are, but would make a very long day unless you resorted to the *astia* technique developed here and in La Gomera of pole-vaulting down mountains (see **Los Tilos Visitors' Centre** for a photo).

The paths are generally good and reasonably well waymarked, though some signposts have already been vandalised, and some paths (notably some of the minor SLs), were never properly cleared – either that or somebody's been chucking the Quick Grow about. If a described path is subject to landslip (notably inside the **Caldera**) or risks disappearing under a barrage of foliage, I will specify in the text.

Apart from the **Caldera mapboards** for official routes through the park, none of the **wayposts** have approximate timings on them, which inevitably makes you wonder if they were actually walked in the first place. To be fair, the waymarking suggests they were, but bear in mind the warning above about the length of some of the 'short' PRs.

Cabildo Mapboards

Except in the north where the ravines have frustrated the road builders, the **GR130** is something of an afterthought, revived after most of the rights of way making up the traditional *Camino Real*, the path's name, had already been asphalted.

However, sufficient imagination has been used in reanimating the way for it to be worthwhile spending a couple of days exploring the human side of La Palma's landscape (see Walks 4&13). The **GR131** (see Walks 6/8/14/27/28/29) on the other hand is a superbly conceived route, following the question mark of crests that define the island. However, it is 110 kilometres long and there are NO hotels, shops or bars en route between **Fuencaliente** and **Puerto Tazacorte**, which would mean carrying three (officially, but more likely four) days worth of food and, at the end, possibly two days' water.

If you wish to do the entire route, ask in the *Medio Ambiente* office (on the second floor of the *Bombas de Agua* building at the southern end of **Santa Cruz**, just before the tunnel) for an *Autorización de Acampada de Traviessa* i.e. permission to camp en route.

The **waymarking symbols** for GRs, PRs, and SLs are the standard:-

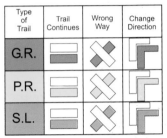

Type of Trail	Trail Continues	Wrong Way	Change Direction
G.R.			
P.R.			
S.L.			

Given that most paths are well waymarked, the **descriptions** are relatively simple. I've tried to give enough detail for those who need confirmation they're on the right path, but not so much as to irritate more confidant pathfinders with superfluity.

Italics are used for discrete Spanish words, also shown in purple where mentioned in the glossary at the back of the book. Place names written on signposts are contained within single quotation marks. **Bold text** is used for street names and place names you may need to show a bus driver if you don't want to end up at the terminal looking foolish. Consistency rather than deficient vocabulary accounts for all **climbs** being 'gentle', 'steady', or 'steep'.

As a general guide a **dirt track** or *pista forestal* indicates something that could be driven, albeit sometimes at a pinch, a **trail** refers to something reasonably broad but better suited to feet, hooves or two wheels rather than four, a **path** is a path, and a **way** either aspires to being a path or was once a path and has long since given up an unequal battle with erosion and/or vegetation.

EQUIPMENT

Unless specified in individual itineraries (for example, Walk 25) nothing out of the ordinary is required, just the customary mountain-walking gear. On the whole you won't have any nasty, unseasonal surprises, but should still carry a windcheater on fine days, and always cover up from the sun when on the high peaks (hat, sunglasses, long-sleeves, suncream etc). Walking boots are preferable to sports shoes, and are essential on the high peaks where it's all rough rock and insidious grit. If you're used to walking poles you'll be glad of them here given the steepness of the island. Also see Walking Equipment on page 27.

Theft, aggressive **dogs** and disagreeable **landowners** are not a problem. **Rockslides** inside the **Caldera** and **forest fires** everywhere are a danger in summer, and there's a small risk of **flash floods** in the *barrancos* during winter, notably in the **Barranco de las Angustias**. If in doubt, ask the park authorities.

The most common problems are strong **winds** on the crests, **mists** in the north, and **dehydration**. Take half a litre of water per person per hour (springs may be dry in summer) and bear in mind that dehydration affects the entire body, including joints and tendons. If you suspect your knees might come in handy in thirty years' time, drink plenty before descending.

Swimming is dangerous, the undertow is strong, people drown. But then nothing so trivial as mortality ever prevented people having fun and everybody swims, despite the dire warnings of the lady in the Tourist Office. Common sense should prevail. Only swim when the sea is calm and you see other people getting in and, preferably, getting out. In high seas even the semi-natural rock pools at **Charco Azul** and **La Fajana** are not secure.

This is not an exhaustive guide, but a resumé of what we noticed and learned in the course of researching the walks.

Monteverde ('green-mountain') is the local name for the dense laurel, wax-myrtle, and heath tree **forests** (also known as *laurisilva*) that cover the northern, north-eastern, and eastern slopes of the island. In the text, I use *laurisilva* in a loose, generic sense, though inevitably the flora, even of superficially similar woodland, is more complex than this suggests. In drier areas the correct term is *fayal-brezal*, a composite of the Spanish words for wax-myrtle and tree-heath.

At lower altitudes, the *laurisilva* is interspersed with chestnut and the occasional walnut. At higher altitudes and in the north-west, Canary Pine dominate though there are some Canary Cedar, too. Along the coast, palms are sufficiently prevalent to be used as brooms by street cleaners.

Another characteristic tree is the *drago* or Dragon Tree, a survivor, like the *laurisilva*, of the last Ice Age, and weird enough to have featured in Hieronymous Bosch's 'Garden of Delights'. You will also see eucalyptus, pepper trees, flamboyants, avocado, fig, orange, apple and pear trees, the last five often run wild.

Of **flowers and shrubs**, look out for rock rose, dog rose, houseleeks, viper's bugloss, violets, gladioli, forget-me-nots, hydrangea, taginaste, cistus and broom, according to altitude, season and orientation.

Prickly pear, as elsewhere in Spain, were long the commonplace alternative to a septic tank and every tiny country cottage (and they are all very tiny) will have its patch to process the household waste. This useful plant not only provided fruit and plumbing, but played host to a flaky white parasite (in evidence on several of our walks) from which cochineal was extracted, a lucrative business before it was superseded by synthetic dyes.

Otherwise, man's biggest impact has been the development of mass banana plantations, which cover the coastal areas, like a gloomy green blanket, only broken up by rough riddled walls erected as windbreaks.

Though the **Caldera de Taburiente** park leaflet claims 25 recorded **bird** species, I can't pretend to have seen anything like that variety myself. Kestrels, chaffinch and rock-doves are common, but perhaps the most emblematic and endearing bird on the island is the chough, with its brilliant orange bill and bright stockinged legs. The sight of a parliament of choughs, chuntering about, chattering and pecking at the ground, like a charabanc party on an outing, is always diverting.

Apart from an inordinate number of dead rats squashed on the road and hordes of diminutive rabbits nervously darting all over the place (with good cause given the gangs of hunters out every weekend with their packs of friendly hunting dogs), the terrestrial **fauna** is limited. We saw one moufflon and that was about it. Ubiquitous, however, is the blue-jowled Canary-lizard. These are the source of the constant rustling in the leaves as you walk along woodland paths. Though frightened of walkers, they are fascinated by picnickers and can become alarmingly inquisitive.

Entomologists will delight in the butterflies which, like the shrubs, attain tropical proportions, and in the tremendous number of dragon flies.

EATING & DRINKING

With plenty of good country restaurants, strong local wines, and shady pine forests, this is the land of a thousand siestas. Imagining a typical meal, you might care to slake your thirst with one of the local beers (*cerveza*), Dorada, Reina, and Tropical, all of which are additive free and, by Spanish standards, excellent.

These might be accompanied by a delicious grilled goat cheese (*queso asado*) brushed with green pepper and/or coriander sauce, *mojo verde*, the classic Canaries sauce that goes well with everything savoury.

Vegetarians will then have to hope there's something based on chick-peas (*garbanzas*), beans (*judias*), or lentils (*lentejas*) without too much meat floating about in it. Otherwise you'll be stuck with the standard salad (*ensalada mixta*), omelette (*tortilla*) and more goat's cheese, unless you're a fish-eater, in which case you could try the local chowder (*sopa de arroz*), or one of the many **fish** (*pescado*) that are either unique to these waters or uniquely named.

Apart from the ubiquitous bream (*dorada*) and hake (*merluza* aka *cherne*), the former farmed the latter wild, few of the local fish will be familiar, but nothing will be quite so strange as *Tollos a la Canaria*. Don't worry if this challenges your Spanish; it challenges the Spanish of mainland Spaniards, too! It's the local word for shark (*tiburón* in Spanish) and once you've tasted it (strong and very fishy), you may begin to appreciate why they took the trouble to rename it.

On the whole though, main courses are **meat** (*carne*) - and very good, too. Nearly everything is raised and fed naturally on the island, so you won't find yourself confronted with a shrivelled lump of leather swimming in a puddle of water, hormones, and antibiotics. Even the beef (*ternera*, *buey*, or *res*), a variety of elderly veal on the mainland, is excellent. But the real specialities are roasted kid (*cabrito*), stewed goat (*cabra con salsa*), rabbit (*conejo*), pork loin and chops (respectively *solomillo* and *chuletas de cerdo*), and to a lesser extent lamb (*cordero*).

Anything that's not stewed will preferably be grilled on an open fire (*a la brasa*) and will undoubtedly be served with more *mojo*, this time *mojo rojo* made with red peppers, and the excellent local potatoes, *papas arrugados*, or 'wrinkled potatoes', boiled in their jackets in sea water or with lots of salt and little water, resulting in a taste and texture that suggests parboiling and baking. A popular and filling snack introduced by migrants returning from Venezuela are *arepas*, thick maize pancakes wrapped round a savoury filling.

By now you will doubtless be getting thirsty again. In small country restaurants, it's generally worthwhile trying the house **wine**, *vino de la casa*, which won't be a fine wine, but will be an experience, usually pleasurable. Red wines tend to be light on colour and heavy on everything else. The best of the reds is Teneguia Negramoll, *negramoll* being one of the island's key grape varieties.

Tea wines are not a remote echo of the temperance movement, but wines matured in barrels made from the heartwood of the Canary pine, also known as *tea*, which gives them a distinctively resinous aftertaste (*tea* is also the wood used for the balconies of traditional La Palman town houses). They're often compared to *retsina*, but might better be described as a dry Madeira laced with thyme. Peculiar, but pleasant.

The white wines are light and fruity and worth trying. The most famous local wine is *Malvasia*, better known in English as Malmsey, a sweet, pleasantly light dessert wine. A dry variety can be found, but isn't worth the search.

Wherever possible, walks end at or near a *típico*, a rated bar or restaurant, but there are a number of extra recommendations in the Appendices.

TOURIST STUFF

La Palma is refreshingly free of the usual tourist circus, but there's plenty to fill a day off walking.

The islanders are very proud of their **petroglyphs**, commonly whorled but occasionally rectilinear symbols carved onto rocks by the pre-hispanic inhabitants, the *Auaritas* (often called *Benahoare*, the island's original name, meaning Land of my Ancestors). There's disagreement about what these carvings mean, some claiming religious symbolism, others the location of springs. On the whole, they're not the most stunning archaeological finds, but evocative enough if you happen to stumble on one in the wild. Most tourists see them in the **Belmaco Cave** (near the end of Walk 4) or **Parque Cultural La Zarza** (see Walks 19&20).

Without forgetting the warning about swimming, it's worth visiting the *piscinas naturales*, or **'natural' swimming pools** at **La Fajana** and **Charco Azul**, below **Barlovento** and **Los Sauces**.

The Tourist Information Office

Ask in the **Tourist Information Office** (housed in the 17th century **Casa de Salazar**) for their free booklet, 'A Historical and Artisitic Guide to Santa Cruz de la Palma' with which you can stroll around the cobbled streets of this quaint and attractive little town. There are plenty of places to stop and take in the architecture and atmosphere over a *cortado* or *cerveza*.

Balconies in Santa Cruz

The wooden balconies seen on many of the older properties are built onto the rear of the buildings. Some of the most photographed are those found facing the sea, their front doors opening onto **Calle Real**.

Strolling round the charming old town of **Santa Cruz**, you're bound to see somebody hand-rolling **cigars** - and probably smoking a Marlboro at the same time. The tobacco industry is in decline, but La Palman cigars have been compared not unfavourably with their Cuban model.

Most of the town's traditional shops are to be found around **Calle Real** and the narrow streets leading off it. If you enjoy searching out unusual keepsakes, this is the place.

Shoe repair shop, Santa Cruz

Several of the town's most historic buildings are open to the public, some housing museums. The Tourist Office and their booklet will guide you to these.

Typical Square, Santa Cruz de La Palma

The Ayuntamiento (Town Hall, 1559)

MARKETS

There's a good fresh produce market (*mercado*) from Mondays to Saturdays, 06.00 - 14.30 in **Santa Cruz de La Palma**, and in **Los Llanos de Aridane** with similar opening hours, and also in **Mazo** on Saturdays and Sundays. But if you want to see something a bit different, it's worth visiting the *Mercadillo* on Saturday afternoons and Sundays (11.00 - 15.00) at **Puntagorda**, where local and not so local artisans and smallholders sell their wares and produce. Ordinary **shopping** is limited; even so, every village seems to have its own little provisions shop, sometimes doubling as a bar, and perhaps a craft shop.

OTHER THINGS TO DO

Even if you're relying on buses for most of your trip, I recommend hiring a car for a day or two, as **driving** round the island gives a different perspective on the place, usually enjoyable, sometimes alarming, notably on minor roads down to the coast.

Ask in the Tourist Information Office about **fiestas** (there's a promotional booklet on the subject) and the numerous **adventure sports** the island boasts, notably diving, climbing, potholing, paragliding, and mountain-biking (see Appendices for details). Some of these are listed in the booklet 'Leisure Activities Guide', from the Tourist Information Office.

The waters around La Palma are ideal for **scuba diving**, with particular interest to be had off the shores near **Fuencaliente** following the 1972 volcanic eruption centred on **Teneguía**. If you want to go **fishing** or whale and dolphin spotting, see the Appendices.

There's a number of **horse riding** organisations, most of which teach riding skills as well as offering treks for capable riders.

There are a couple of **parachuting/paragliding** clubs (*parapenting*) who train beginners as well as taking on the experienced.

Mountain bikers will find hire shops as well as cycling clubs to provide equipment and advice, or the chance to join groups.

With its wealth of volcanic tubes, underground chambers and caves , La Palma is a haven for **caving**. The cave of **Todoque** is the island's best known, and is one of its longest. It also lays claim to unusual endemic fauna.

The **Parque Botánico y Faunístico Maroparque** in **Breña Alta** is the place to find out more about the island's **flora and fauna**. There's also a small zoo and aquarium, along with the usual tourist-style shop, bar and café. **Parque Paraíso de las Aves** (Paradise park for Birdlife) in **El Paso** has a wider brief than birds alone, featuring plants and wildife and with a declared interest in the preservation and protection of endangered species.

Observatorio de El Roque

If the heavens are your thing, visits to the **Observatory** at **Roque de Los Muchachos** can be arranged; ask in the Tourist Information Office or contact **Agrupación Astronómica de La Palma** (AAP), details in the Appendices.

ACKNOWLEDGEMENTS

After four books, the thanks are becoming customary, but no less heartfelt: to Jeannette for doing all the dirty jobs; to Ros and David for doing all the boring ones; to Bati for being discretely illicit despite extreme feline provocation; and to the *Medio Ambiente* people who labour against the weekend litter machine.

LOCATION MAPS

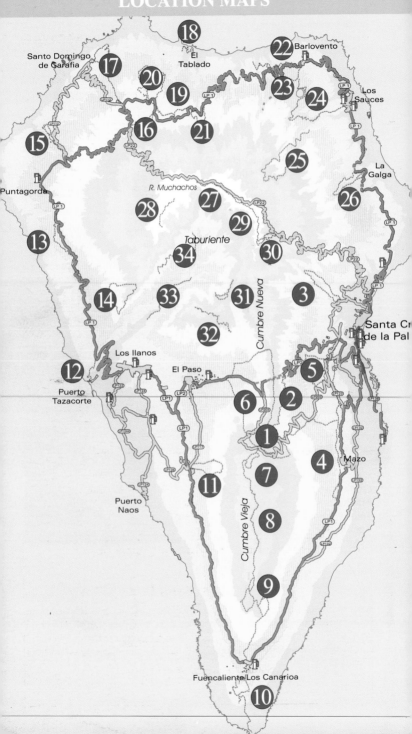

The Canary Islands lie approximately 100 kilometres west of North Africa's Atlantic Coast, and approximately 1100 kilometres south-west of the Spanish Mainland.

SPAIN

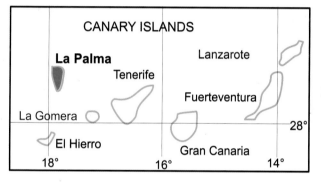

CANARY ISLANDS

La Palma

Lanzarote

Tenerife

Fuerteventura

La Gomera

28°

El Hierro

Gran Canaria

18°   16°   14°

The map sections used in this book have been adapted from:

La Palma Tour & Trail Super-Durable 1:40,000 scale Map
ISBN 1-904946-07-0

published by

Discovery Walking Guides Ltd.
10 Tennyson Close
Northampton NN5 7HJ, England
www.walking.demon.co.uk
www.dwgwalking.co.uk

The map sections used in our **Walk! La Palma** walk descriptions are taken from **La Palma Tour & Trail Super-Durable Map** published by **Discovery Walking Guides Ltd**.

To improve the clarity of each map section the waypoints of adjoining routes have been 'switched off' before making the map section so as to avoid any confusion that might arise if we showed all the waypoints for all the routes covered by that map. The result is that the map for a walking route only shows the waypoints for that walking route along its route. You can see the benefits of this detailed approach when comparing the maps for routes with common sections; such as Walk 29 and Walk 30 where **Pico de la Nieve** is Waypoint 10 in Walk 29 and Waypoint 6 in Walk 30.

La Palma Tour & Trail Super-Durable Map is a 1:40,000 scale map, printed on special high density polymer coated with a heat-fused china clay surface. The result is a map that feels like silk but is Super-Durable; we really do mean Super-Durable as the map is waterproof, tearproof and almost everything-proof to survive the toughest of outdoor conditions.

La Palma Tour & Trail Super-Durable Map £7.99
ISBN 1904946070
is available from book shops or post free from:-

Discovery Walking Guides Ltd
10 Tennyson Close
Northampton NN5 7HJ
England

www.walking.demon.co.uk & www.dwgwalking.co.uk

La Palma Tour & Trail Legend-Legende

ALTITUDE, HÖHE, ALTITUD, ALTITUDE

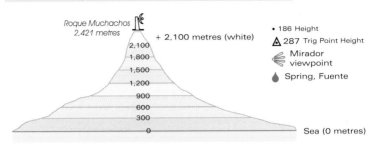

Roque Muchachos
2,421 metres

+ 2,100 metres (white)

2,100
1,800
1,500
1,200
900
600
300
0

Sea (0 metres)

- • 186 Height
- ▲ 287 Trig Point Height
- Mirador viewpoint
- ◆ Spring, Fuente

ROADS, STRAßE, CARRETERA, ROUTE

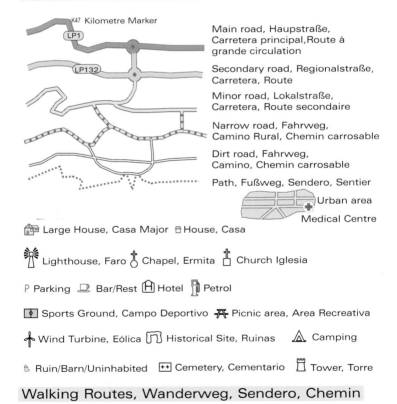

K47 Kilometre Marker

LP1

LP132

Main road, Haupstraße, Carretera principal, Route à grande circulation

Secondary road, Regionalstraße, Carretera, Route

Minor road, Lokalstraße, Carretera, Route secondaire

Narrow road, Fahrweg, Camino Rural, Chemin carrosable

Dirt road, Fahrweg, Camino, Chemin carrosable

Path, Fußweg, Sendero, Sentier

Urban area

Medical Centre

Large House, Casa Major House, Casa

Lighthouse, Faro Chapel, Ermita Church Iglesia

P Parking Bar/Rest Hotel Petrol

Sports Ground, Campo Deportivo Picnic area, Area Recreativa

Wind Turbine, Eólica Historical Site, Ruinas Camping

Ruin/Barn/Uninhabited Cemetery, Cementario Tower, Torre

Walking Routes, Wanderweg, Sendero, Chemin

Walk! La Palma Route (Red) 17

GPS Waypoint
see Walk! La Palma
Waypoint Lists

8

our rating for effort/exertion:-
1 very easy **2** easy **3** average
4 energetic **5** strenuous

 approximate **time** to complete a walk (compare your times against ours early in a walk) - does not include stopping time

 approximate walking **distance** in kilometres

 approximate **ascents/descents** in metres (N = negligible)

 circular route

linear route

risk of **vertigo**

 refreshments rating refers to the quality of refreshment opportunities, not the number of choices (may be at start or end of a route only)

Notes: Access by taxi
TF = 'taxi-friendly' i.e. car-access walks feasible and affordable by taxi; **TF$** = feasible but expensive (€30+); **4X4T** = feasible but probably only accepted by 4X4 taxis.

Walk descriptions include:

- timing in minutes, shown as (40M)
- compass directions, shown as (NW)
- heights in metres, shown as (1355m)
- GPS waypoints, shown as (Wp.3)

Notes on the text
Place names are shown in **bold text**, except where we refer to a written sign, when any place names are enclosed in single quotation marks.

Spanish words are shown in *italics*, and if also in *purple*, will be included in the glossary (P.xxx).

Waymarked walking routes referred to in the text include:-
Gran Recorridos (GR) or long-distance footpaths,
Pequeño Recorridos (PR) or 'short' distance footpaths and
Senderos Locales (SL) See P.10 for further details.

The GPS Waypoint lists provided in this **Walk! La Palma** guide book by Charles Davis, are as recorded during the research of the 34 main walk descriptions contained in the book. In the interests of clarity, not all waypoints included in these lists are shown on the maps which accompany each detailed walk description. Where a Waypoint symbol is shown on a map it is numbered so that it can be directly identified against the walk description and waypoint list.

All The GPS Waypoints quoted in **Walk! La Palma** were recorded during the research of the walking routes, and are subject to the general considerations as to the accuracy of GPS units in the location concerned. Arriving on the world's steepest island you soon realise that the deep *barrancos* and extensive pine forest make for potentially poor GPS reception. In the **Los Tilos** biosphere reserve, Walk 25, the severe landscape conspires with tunnels and forest to make GPS navigation impossible with any degree of accuracy; similar conditions preclude GPS use on Walk 26 and for these two routes you should stay with the detailed walk description.

Given La Palma's dramatic landscape GPS reception is surprisingly good for the majority of our walking routes. Routes where poor GPS reception was experienced are; Walk 2 at start, Walk 3 at top of *barranco* Wps. 5 to 9, Walk 9 until Wp.2, Walk 13 after Wp.17, Walk 18, Walk 19 between Wps.13 to 14 and 16 to 19, Walk 20 poor after Wp.8, Walk 24 good from Wp.2 to 10 then poor to 14 then good to 17, Walk 30 poor at start until Wp.2, Walk 33 variable reception due to the *barranco* walls, Walk 34 reasonable reception but follow the detailed walk description with GPS as a check.

It is virtually impossible to reproduce the exact GPS Waypoint co-ordinates in practice when walking a route. While GPS Waypoints are quoted to 00.0001 minutes of arc, in practice you should expect 10 metres as an acceptable standard of accuracy when you have '3D navigation' (four or more satellites in view).

Signal Strength
Signal strength from sufficient satellites is crucial to obtaining an accurate location fix with your GPS unit. In open sky, ridge top, conditions you may have up to 11 satellites in view to give you a GPS location accuracy of 5 metres. Providing you have good batteries, and that you wait until your GPS has full 'satellite acquisition' before starting out, your GPS will perform well on La Palma for the majority of our walking routes.

To Input the Waypoints
GPS Waypoint co-ordinates are quoted for the WGS84 datum, in degrees and minutes of Latitude and Longitude. To input the Waypoints into your GPS we suggest that you:-

- switch on your GPS and select 'simulator' mode.
- check that your GPS is set to the WGS84 datum (its default datum) and the 'location format' 'hddd° .mm.mmm'.
- input the GPS Waypoints into a 'route' file with the same number as the walking route number; then when you call up the 'route' on La

Palma there will be no confusion as to which walking route it refers.

- repeat the inputting of routes until you have covered all the routes you plan to walk, or until you have used up the memory capacity of your GPS; even the most basic of GPS units will store up to 20 routes of up to 50 Waypoints for each route, and you can always re-programme your GPS while on La Palma.
- turn off your GPS. When you turn the GPS back on it should return to its normal navigation mode.
- Note that GPS Waypoints complement the detailed walking route descriptions in Walk! La Palma; and are not intended as an alternative to the detailed walking route description.

Personal Navigator Files (PNFs) CD version 2.01
Edited versions of the original GPS research tracks and waypoints are available as downloadable files on our **PNFs CD**. In addition to **La Palma** the CD contains **Tenerife**, **La Gomera**, **Lanzarote**, **Mallorca**, **Menorca**, **Madeira**, **Andorra**, **Axarquia**, **Aracena** and **Alpujarras**; plus GPS Utility Special Edition software and examples from our **Walk! UK** series of guidebooks. See DWG websites for more information:

www.walking.demon.co.uk **&** www.dwgwalking.co.uk

Confused by GPS?
If you are confused by talk of GPS, but are interested in how this modern navigational aid could enhance your walking enjoyment, then simply seek out a copy of **GPS The Easy Way**, the UK's best selling GPS manual. Written in an easy to read, lively, style and lavishly illustrated, **GPS The Easy Way** takes you through all aspects of GPS usage from absolute basics up to GPS Expert and debunking the myths about GPS along the way; an essential purchase for anyone thinking of buying a GPS.

"A compass points north"
but
"A GPS tells you where you are, where you have been, and can show you where you want to go."

"Ask not 'What is GPS?' - ask 'What can GPS do for me?'"

GPS The Easy Way (£4.99) is available from bookshops, outdoor shops, over the internet, and post free from:

Discovery Walking Guides Ltd.
10 Tennyson Close
Northampton NN5 7HJ
www.walking.demon.co.uk **&** www.dwgwalking.co.uk

From reading the postings on uk.rec.walking internet news group, it's obvious that walkers are most interested in the clothing and equipment used by other walkers. For some this interest borders on obsession, with heated debates over walking poles, boots versus sandals, GPS versus 'map and compass' navigation etc. etc. Walking magazines are packed with clothing and equipment reviews, opinions and adverts, but few walking guide books give more than a cursory mention to recommended clothing and equipment.

Having chosen La Palma for a walking vacation you are probably an experienced walker with your own opinions of what is 'good gear'. At the risk of upsetting some walking fundamentalists, here is a brief rundown on our recommendations for La Palma.

BACKPACK

A 25-30 litre day pack should easily cope with all the equipment you think you will need for a day's walking. A design with plenty of outside pockets to give easy access to frequently used items, such as ½ litre water bottles, is a good starting point. Well padded straps will spread the load and a waist strap will stop the pack moving about on the more adventurous routes. A ventilated back panel will help clear sweat on hot days and tough routes; a design with a stand-off frame is best for ventilation and worth the small increase in weight. Do spend time adjusting the straps so that you get the most comfortable fit.

As an alternative to traditional backpack designs, you might find the cyclist's packs produced by Nikko, and similar companies, a good compromise of stand-off frame, capacity, pockets and weight.

FOOTWEAR

Whether you choose boots, shoes or sandals they must be up to the task. You will need a hard sole with plenty of grip and a well padded foot-bed. Charles uses Bestard boots and I (David Brawn) can recommend the Bestard Race K shoes worn with thick mountain socks. Bestard boots and shoes are not widely available in UK, but if you happen to visit Mallorca call in at their factory shop in Lloseta. Ros Brawn likes Cat sandals for La Palma's rough trails, or the toughest of the Merrell designs for less rugged paths.

Whichever footwear you choose, do make sure that you have covered plenty of kilometres in them before coming to La Palma. Blisters and sores can ruin your walking experience.

SUN PROTECTION

La Palma might be the wettest Canary Island, but you should be prepared for the sun at any time of year. Wear comfortable loose clothing and always carry a comfortable sun hat. Choose a design that gives you plenty of shade, is comfortable to wear, and stays on your head in windy conditions; our choice is the Rohan 'Legionnaire' style which protects neck and ears. The author of this book (Charles Davis) favours the legendary Tilley design (the one that apparently passes unscathed through an elephant's digestive tract!) As you'll be spending several hours a day outdoors, there's a high risk of sunburnt ears and neck, both of which are painful and embarrassing. Use a high-factor sun cream on all exposed skin.

We favour wrap-round sunglasses which, as well as reducing UV radiation, protect from getting grit in our eyes on windy days. When you do take a break, always choose to sit in the shade if any is available.

WATER & FOOD

Dehydration is a real danger on the longer, more energetic routes. Always carry as much water as you think you might drink. A couple of ½ litre bottles, a few pence each from local shops, is the minimum, and add extra for longer routes. Before starting out, drink as much water as you comfortably can, and at the end of your route, drink water before rewarding yourself with that beer.

Even on shorter routes, we would advise that you carry some survival rations. Chocolate bars and the like can provide welcome comfort when out in the wild, though wrap well against melting into the rest of your kit. Bananas are a good, quick acting energy pick-me-up.

MEDICAL KIT

Antiseptic wipes, antiseptic cream, tissues, plasters and bandage are supplemented by lip salve. Also include tweezers, which you will soon appreciate if you catch a splinter or cactus spine, and a whistle to attract attention if you get into difficulties.

NAVIGATION

Do not compromise - buy the best guide book and the best map, and carry them with you. A compass is useful to orientate yourself at the start of a route and for general directions, but a GPS unit is far more useful - see Using GPS on La Palma.

CLOTHING

Choose loose comfortable clothing and add a lightweight waterproof jacket to your back pack. La Palma has a diversity of landscapes ranging from the exposed volcanic south of the **Cumbre Nueva**, through the unique **Caldera de Taburiente**, up to the high altitude rim of the *caldera* and on to the forest and farmland of the north. La Palma might be a Canary Island but you will appreciate packing some warm clothing for winter nights.

OTHER EQUIPMENT

You won't want to be carrying excess weight during your walking, especially on the longer routes with major ascents/descents. Digital cameras weigh far less than their film equivalents, and a monocular is half the weight of a pair of binoculars. A mobile phone, and money (refreshments, taxis, public telephones, drinks machines etc.) are also recommended.

1 MONTEVERDE

An ideal introduction to the flora of the *monteverde* or 'green mountain', the local name for the jungle-like *laurisilva* forests of the highlands. Following waymarked trails, we climb through classic *monteverde* to the pine fringed spine of the island, the **Cumbre Nueva**, then return to the popular **Pared Vieja** *área recreativa* via a lovely donkey trail.

Access: by car or TF (see P.20)
Drivers park in the *área recreativa* car-park.

Extension
If arriving by taxi, see Walk 2 Wp.10+ or Walk 6 Wp.7+ for the descent.

Pared Vieja

Our walk starts opposite the entrance to the **Pared Vieja** *área recreativa* on the **San Isidro-El Pilar** road, next to a vandalised signpost for the **PR18** (Wp.1 0M). Ignoring a path to the left, we take the dirt track on the right, the green-and-white waymarked **SL132**, which winds through the woods, passing a branch to **El Pajead de Charuco** (Wp.2 15M).

At a Y-junction (Wp.3 20M), we ignore a green-gated track to the left and take the red-barred track to the right, climbing across abandoned terraces with fine views along the coast and over to Tenerife. The track becomes increasingly overgrown and eventually dwindles to a path. Turning left at a T-junction with a clear dirt track then, almost immediately, right, we join the **PR17** (Wp.4 30M). Ignoring three branches to the left, we follow the yellow-and-white waymarks of the PR, climbing steadily to steeply, crossing a dirt track, and passing a small white cross and a signposted branch of the **SL124** (Wp.5 40M).

Turning right at the junction with the **Pista Camino de la Faya** (Wp.6 45M), we pass a *mirador* with an explanatory picture-board about the *monteverde*. After a large bungalow, we bear right (Wp.7 50M) on the dusty **Pista General** or **Pista El Cabrito**, which runs along the eastern flank of the **Cumbre Vieja**. Crossing a wooden footbridge (Wp.8 53M), we climb steeply on a narrow, shady, shortcut path before rejoining the dirt track (Wp.9 55M). Fifteen metres to the right we leave the track again, turning left to continue on our shady path as it runs parallel to the road, again climbing steeply before levelling off as the *monteverde* merges with pine.

Crossing the road (Wp.10 60M), we continue through dense woods, passing a picture-board about the *faya* or wax-myrtle. After another brief climb, the

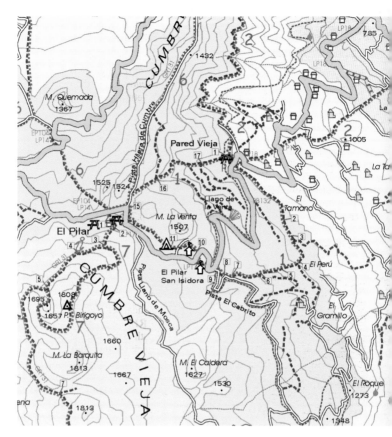

path levels out and becomes a broad walking trail meandering through the pine, crossing first the **Pista Hoyo de Rehielo** (Wp.11 65M) then a wooden footbridge (Wp.12 67M). Bearing left up a minor forestry track, we ignore a branch to the left and cross a second footbridge (Wp.13 70M) onto another path that soon joins the road (Wp.14 73M). After following the road through a long bend, we bear right on a broad dirt track, the **Pista Hilera de la Cumbre** (Wp.15 80M), 100 metres above the **Pilar Refuge** and camping area. Ten metres behind the 'Comienzo Municipio Breña Alta' panel, we bear right on a narrow path, PR-waymarked but not signposted, descending through the trees.

The path, which to begin with is slippery with pine needles, passes a **PR18** signpost for **Los Guinchos** (Wp.16 90M), after which the pine gradually gives way to *laurisilva*. Tunnelling through the woods, we descend steadily on a shady, partially paved trail lined with ancient, mossy cairns. Emerging from the tree cover, we traverse large blocks of rock to a junction with a dirt track below a small shrine (Wp.17 105M). Crossing the track, we follow a clearly waymarked path down to Wp.1.

2 PISTA DE LOS LOMOS - MONTAÑA DE LA BREÑA - SAN JOSÉ

A long, easy walk serving as an excellent introduction to the flora of La Palma <u>and</u> the local transport system! Snaking along below the **Cumbre Nueva**, we pass through dense *laurisilva* to the **Pared Vieja Área Recreativa**, set amid fine Canary pine. En route we see shrubs the size of bushes, bushes the size of trees, and get a slightly gamey whiff of decaying vegetation reminiscent of the forests of West Africa. Descending on one of the old donkey trails that were once the only land link between the two sides of the island, we cross largely abandoned farmland with fine views of the countryside south of **Santa Cruz**. There are so many junctions that the descent inevitably sounds confusing, but the waymarking is adequate and the route fairly obvious on the ground.

*in **San José**

Stroll (for motorists / from **Pared Vieja**)	**Short Version** (for motorists / from **Pared Vieja**)
Turn left at the yellow building after the car-park, and keep bearing left, following the track/firebreak round the *Área Recreativa*.	**Pista de los Lomos**
	Extension: Walk 1

Access: by bus
N°s L1 & L3 (from **Santa Cruz**; the bus from **Los Llanos** uses a newer tunnel lower down). Ask for **Túnel de la Cumbre** and, if any doubt is expressed, **Pista de los Lomos a Pared Vieja**. There's no official stop, but plenty of space for pulling over.

Our itinerary starts on a tarmac track (S) between a green electricity substation and a signboard for 'Parque Natural Cumbre Vieja' (Wp.1 0M). The tarmac gives way to dirt after fifty metres and we climb gently, passing a number of secluded spots evidently popular with young couples who have a car but no bed. Fortunately, the detritus doesn't last long and we are soon surrounded by lush vegetation.

The track levels off below shallow cliffs capped with masses of laurel (Wp.2 15M) and, at the next bend (Wp.3 20M), we see Tenerife and La Gomera. Shortly after a rockspill with a pair of rough boulder 'stools' (Wp.4 30M), we pass a sheer cliff with a potted begonia commemorating a German tourist (Wp.5 33M) and climb very slightly, winding into a gully packed with towering laurel and carpeted with dead leaves (Wp.6 45M). Passing a second rockspill, distinguished by the stump of a fallen tree (Wp.7 65M), we again climb very slightly to an exposed stretch in sight of the northernmost volcanoes on the **Cumbre Vieja** (Wp.8 80M) (see Walks 7&8). The laurel

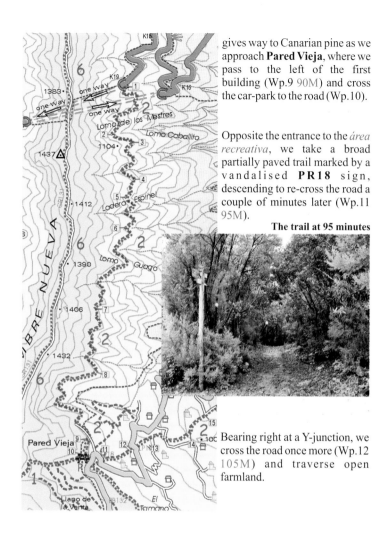

gives way to Canarian pine as we approach **Pared Vieja**, where we pass to the left of the first building (Wp.9 90M) and cross the car-park to the road (Wp.10).

Opposite the entrance to the *área recreativa*, we take a broad partially paved trail marked by a vandalised **PR18** sign, descending to re-cross the road a couple of minutes later (Wp.11 95M).

The trail at 95 minutes

Bearing right at a Y-junction, we cross the road once more (Wp.12 105M) and traverse open farmland.

After crossing a dirt track (Wp.13 110M), we descend to a tarmac lane where the **PR18.2** bears left for 'El Llanito' and we turn right for 'Los Guinchos'. When the tarmac lane becomes a dirt track (Wp.14 120M), we bear left (NE), recovering the old trail and resuming our steady descent.

Joining a narrow, partially overgrown track, we bear right, descending to a concrete track (Wp.15 125M). Bearing right again, we maintain direction (NE) for fifty metres down to a staggered crossroads. Immediately after the first left-hand branch, we turn left on a waymarked path, briefly recovering the donkey trail before passing a small green house (Wp.16 130M), where concrete resumes. Ten metres before the concrete gives way to tarmac, we bear right (Wp.17 135M), recovering the donkey trail and descending, first towards a small green pylon, then between retaining walls toward a large farm backed by a paddock shaded by large chestnut trees.

Crossing the farm driveway (Wp.18 145M) we follow a dirt track between the farm and the **El Pilar** road to a large bank of bindweed, where the **PR18** forks left onto the road for 'Los Guinchos' (Wp.19 150M). Staying on the dirt track, now the **PR18.1** or **Camino de la Ratona**, we head east (E) for 'Montaña de la Breña/Cancajos', circling a well-fenced house patrolled by a couple of humourless looking dogs. Ignoring all branch tracks (including one signposted 'Montaña de la Breña'), we stick to the main dirt track. Shortly after glimpsing a garden of remembrance on our left, we turn left at a T-junction (Wp.20 170M), descending to the cemetery car-park.

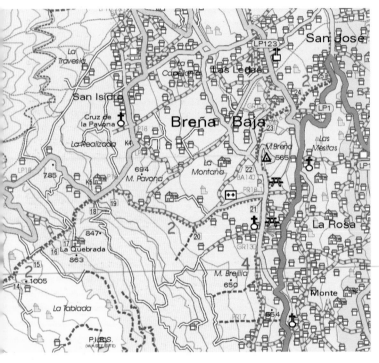

Following the cemetery road down to a T-junction, we turn left on the **GR130** (Wp.21 180M), passing an *área recreativa*, fifty metres after which, the road climbs to **Montaña de la Breña** and we fork left on a GR-signposted walking trail (Wp.22 185M). The trail runs into a dirt track descending to a junction (Wp.23 190M) where the **GR130** continues in a northerly direction and we bear right for 'Cancajos'. Our narrow path soon crosses the **Canal del Estado**, then descends to the **San Pedro** road (Wp.24 195M). Fifty metres to the north, just after house N°90, we turn right on a broad 'Pista Privada' concrete track. After climbing briefly, the track descends between houses and dwindles to a narrow dirt path, briefly interrupted by a thirty metre stretch of concrete track before reaching the **San José** road (Wp.25 205M). Bearing left, we follow the road into **San José**, for refreshments and bus N°L3 back to **Santa Cruz**.

3 BARRANCO DE LA MADERA

On the official map of La Palma's paths, the **PR2.3** looks like nothing much at all. Don't be deceived. This is very much 'something', far and away the most adventurous <u>and</u> riskiest walk in the book. The **Barranco de la Madera** is a bit grim at the beginning, dry, dusty, degraded and dispiriting, but as we climb, the walls of the ravine rise above us, the silence deepens, and we are suffused with a growing sense of isolation, the uncanny hush broken only by the occasional bird, the only other walker, a disgruntled moufflon disdainfully stalking away up an almost vertical cliff. Then, just when it seems things can't get any wilder, we reach our sensational return route, following the **Galería de la Madera**, channelling water through a series of tunnels down to **Santa Cruz**. And it all starts a short bus ride from the town centre at one of the island's top tourist attractions, the seventeenth century **Santuario de las Nieves**.

So why isn't it thronged with walkers? The reason is simple: between the tunnels we teeter along a narrow canal path above sheer drops. It is VERY vertiginous, potentially very dangerous, and should NOT be undertaken by the inexperienced or those who dislike heights. DO NOT do this walk alone or when it's wet underfoot. A pocket torch is useful, but not indispensable. At the time of writing, the path is waymarked but not signposted.

*at the Sanctuary bar

Access: by car and bus N°L10.
If possible, park in the shady alley behind the Sanctuary. Otherwise there's ample parking in the new terraced car-park just above it.

Short Version
To Wp.5 or the 120M point, returning the same way.

We start from the **Sanctuary Plaza de las Nieves** (Wp.1 0M) on a stone stairway in front of the **Bar/Restaurante Parilla las Nieves**. The stairs run into a cobbled alley descending to the sanctuary access road, at the bottom of which, we cross the main road just north of the tunnel. Bearing right toward a breeze-block cabin, we take a dusty dirt track up the left bank of the **Barranco de la Madera**.

The Sanctuary Plaza de las Nieves

Climbing steadily, we cross the watercourse (Wp.2 10M), after which the track becomes stonier and less dusty. The *barranco* narrows as we continue to climb, passing a kennel of hunting dogs tucked into the cliffs to the north.

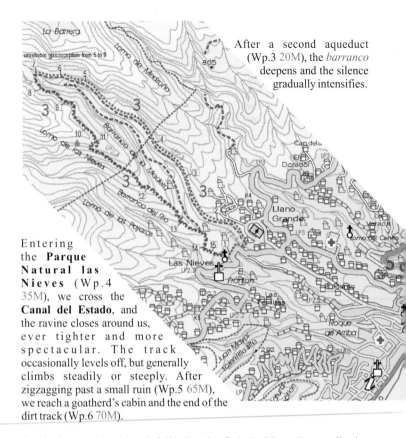

After a second aqueduct (Wp.3 20M), the *barranco* deepens and the silence gradually intensifies.

Entering the **Parque Natural las Nieves** (Wp.4 35M), we cross the **Canal del Estado**, and the ravine closes around us, ever tighter and more spectacular. The track occasionally levels off, but generally climbs steadily or steeply. After zigzagging past a small ruin (Wp.5 65M), we reach a goatherd's cabin and the end of the dirt track (Wp.6 70M).

Continuing on a broad path following the **Galería Mercedes** canalisation pipe, we climb into the depths of the *barranco*, where apart from the occasional roar of water, the silence is absolute – also absolute is the absence of satellite coverage for GPS, hence no waypoints. Like the track before it, the path passes occasional level stretches, but on the whole, climbs steadily, passing a slightly vertiginous stretch under an overhang. After the third level stretch, we pass through a rock archway (90M) leading to another slightly vertiginous section. A fourth level stretch leads to the mouth of a deep tunnel (100M) (a delightfully fresh bolt-hole in hot weather) littered with mining trolley-cars and rails.

We have now reached the last stretch of our climb. Taking a steep, slippery path to the right of the tunnel, we leave the **Galería Mercedes** and, thirty metres later, cross back onto the left bank of the *barranco*. The path here is rougher and slightly overgrown, but always visible and well waymarked, as it climbs steeply to what appears to be an impenetrable wall of rock. Had it not been for the engineers, it would have been! Pressing on, always climbing, always heading west up the *barranco* (there's nowhere else to go) we finally come to the foot of a huge dry waterfall. There's a small stone bridge to the right and, on our left, the first tunnel along the *galería* (120M).

This is where sufferers of vertigo have to decide how badly they want to do the full loop. The worst sections come after the first (a narrow path with an inconveniently bulging wall) and second (a long narrow stretch over sheer drops) tunnels.

At first, the tunnel looks dismal, but after a few metres a 'window' brightens the way. Crouching low, we creep along, eventually emerging on the first very vertiginous stretch (130M), which is mercifully short, only lasting some 75 metres before we get to the second tunnel. The path after the second tunnel (135M) is narrower, but marginally less vertiginous thanks to shrubbery and trees, which act as 'blinkers' shielding us from the drop. The third tunnel (Wp.7 140M) is only a few metres long. We now reach more densely wooded land and, though there are one or two vertiginous stretches, the worst is over. If you've coped so far, there's nothing much to worry about anymore, apart from braining yourself in the fourth tunnel (Wp.8 150M), where the roof occasionally dips down unexpectedly. A final stroll through an alley of laurel (Wp.9 160M) leads to a large water tower (Wp.10 170M) where our descent begins.

Briefly bearing left, away from the water pipe, we zigzag down to rejoin it a little way below. One hundred metres later (Wp.11 175M), another zigzagging path takes us away from the *galería* (S) onto the **Lomo de las Nieves**, which divides the **Barrancos de la Madera** and **de las Nieves**. From here, the major part of the descent is straightforward as we follow a steep path down through the pine, largely on the southern side of the *lomo* with steadily improving views of the countryside behind **Santa Cruz**. The only slightly confusing point is when the path swings left, back towards **Barranco de la Madera**, and an old, faded cross indicates we leave the main path and take a faint branch to the right (Wp.12 200M). Ignore the cross and stay on the main path. Soon after this we see the Mirca sports stadium.

Ignoring two minor branches up the **Barranco de las Nieves**, we follow a *galería* for 75 metres before bearing right (SE) (Wp.13 220M) to continue our steady descent. Passing a house with a large pond/reservoir and a garden packed with palm trees, we emerge on a small plateau, where we bear right on a grassy path passing between two small ruins. Crossing a concrete track (Wp.14 230M), we bear left on a broad dirt trail down to a dry reservoir (Wp.15 235M) where we bear left again to descend into the large new car-park (currently ploughed terraces, but presumably completed by the time you read this) immediately behind the sanctuary and our starting point.

4 THE GOOD, THE HIGH, THE LOW & THE BAD

If you're seeking wild places and dislike tarmac, read no further; there are other routes in this book for you. If, on the other hand, you want a blast of fresh air on a blustery winter's day when wild places might be a tad too wild, the **GR130** is ideal. Starting with the 'good', **Buenavista**, we visit the 'high' and 'low' of the **Breñas Alta** and **Baja**, then take the **PR16.1** down to the 'bad country' of **Malpais**.

Buenavista is home to the old airport and the **Mirador de la Concepción** overlooking **Santa Cruz**; **Breña Alta** or **San Pedro** is the nucleus of the declining cigar manufactories and boasts the island's most famous Dragon Trees, the twin **Dragos Gemelos**; **Breña Baja** or **San José** developed round the seventeenth century church of the same name, built to minister to the farming community, and is now the administrative hub of La Palma's emerging tourism industry; finally, **Malpais**, a windswept volcanic landscape so inhospitable its hapless residents were reduced to the desperate measure of cultivating grapes for malmsey! The roads are peaceful lanes, apart from the climb past **Ermita de San Miguel**. The plethora of lanes and tracks make the route sound complicated, but the waymarking is clear, except in built up areas. The 'average' exertion rating is due to the length.

| 3 | 3¼ H | 14 km | 250m 400m one way | 3* |

* in Malpais

Access by bus

N°s L1 or L91 & L7. The bus stops are 100 metres north of Wp.1 and fifty metres north of Wp.24.

Short Versions

To avoid the built up area, taxi to **Montaña de la Breña** (Wp.10) or take the bus N°L3 to **San José** and follow Walk 2 in reverse to the dirt track between Wps.9&10.

Our start point at the 'gate'

We start in **Buenavista Abajo** at the symbolic 'gate' of curving metal pillars perched on the raised intersection of the **Breña Alta** road and the LP2 to **Los Llanos** (Wp.1 0M). If you haven't yet visited it, it's worth detouring north 100 metres to climb the **Mirador de la Concepción**. For the main walk, we follow the **Breña Alta** road (S) and, just before a U-turn roundabout, fork left into an alley alongside the main road. Crossing a side road, we pass house N°58 on a concrete, then tarmac lane, the **Camino Real**, which we follow into **San Pedro**, briefly rejoining the main road en route (Wp.2 5M). As the lane climbs into town, we maintain direction (S), passing the Ayumar electrical wholesalers and **Calle Espinel**. Approaching the church, we bear left on **Calle del Cura** (Wp.3 14M) then cross the **San José** road onto **Calle Luis Wandevalle**. When this swings left, we maintain our southerly direction on a concrete then cobbled track, **Calle Cuesta La Pata**, which descends out of the urban area into **Barranco del Llanito**.

In the *barranco*, we cross a tarmac lane and grassy wasteland to join a busy backroad (Wp.4 25M) climbing steeply (S) to the **San Miguel** chapel before gradually levelling out. After passing the **Caminos a Calafata** and **Los Brezos** and a large equestrian centre, we see our next objective, **Montaña de la Breña** with its distinctive crooked cross visible on the peak. When the backroad joins the main road (Wp.5 40M), we bear left onto a quieter lane behind a vivid pink house, eventually crossing the main road in front of a large house (N°84) topped with a flagpole (Wp.6 45M).

When the lane swings right at house N°22 (Wp.7 50M), we continue straight ahead on a concrete track leading to another lane (Wp.8 55M). Turning left then sharp right forty metres later, we follow a third lane to a junction next to a **Breña Baja** tourist information board. Bearing right, we climb to a Y-junction (Wp.9 60M) and fork right on a waymarked concrete track.

When the track swings right, we climb past a water-hut and clamber onto the **Canal del Estado**. Bearing left, we follow the canal round to a road and take a concrete track for **Mazo**. A short, steep climb brings us onto dirt track, where we join the **PR18.1** (see Walk 2). Climbing the track, we pass in front of a bright orange house and continue climbing steadily on a broad dirt trail, joining **Carrer de la Montaña** below **Montaña de la Breña** (Wp.10 75M).

Maintaining direction (S), we follow **Carrer de la Montaña** past the **Montaña de la Breña Área Recreativa** and the turn off for the **PR18.1**, after which we have excellent views out to sea and along the coast. Climbing past the **Cuesta Anselmo** and a small *mirador*, we follow **Carrer de la Montaña** till it swings left and we continue straight ahead on a minor lane (Wp.11 90M). The lane climbs steeply for fifty metres before levelling off then climbing again and running into a partially cobbled track. The track runs between well-maintained walls, passing an idyllic little tumbledown farm with a characteristically tall, wind-cheating La Palman chimney (Wp.12 100M).

Joining a narrow lane (Wp.13 105M), we cross the **PR17** and continue on an intermittently metalled track into the outskirts of **Mazo**. When the asphalted **Camino El Poleal** swings left, we continue straight ahead on the **Camino Las Toscas** dirt track (Wp.14 120M), passing below a small *área recreativa*, immediately after which the track becomes a tarmac lane and the **PR16** branches left into **Mazo** (Wp.15 130M). **Camino Las Toscas** eventually joins the newly surfaced LP121 (Wp.16 135M), which we follow (S) till it swings down toward the main road and we bear right for **Los Canarios**. After traversing a dry watercourse and passing behind a large reservoir, we cross a dirt track, and continue on a slightly overgrown path running along a terrace, which gradually broadens to a rough dirt track descending to a small *fuente/área recreativa* next to the main road (Wp.17 145M).

Continuing on a gently sloping lane parallel to the road, we bear left just after the second branch on the right, taking another overgrown path, also parallel to the road. The path gradually bears away from the road, climbing gently before levelling out near the straggly hamlet of **La Salina** and crossing a concrete track (Wp.18 155M). Climbing alongside a gully, we cross a lane, ten metres above which we bear left, crossing the gully onto a donkey trail leading to another tarmac lane (Wp.19 160M), on which the GR is joined by the **PR16.1** from **Roque Niquiomo**. The two paths follow the lane until a small shrine (on our left) with a blue background and white stars (Wp.20 170M), where we turn left, leaving the GR and descending on a broad cobbled way.

The cobbled way runs into a road, which we follow till it swings left and we continue straight ahead on more cobbles.

Passing under the main road to **Fuencaliente** (Wp.21 180M), we join a tiny tarmac lane and continue descending with fine views over the coast. Ten metres after the tarmac gives way to concrete, we bear right to recover the cobbled way. After a steep descent, we turn right on a minor road (Wp.22 185M), which we follow to a classic La Palman 'dalmatian' house (N°104) (Wp.23 200M) where we bear left, leaving the road to descend on a waymarked concrete then dirt track that brings us into **Malpais** next to the **Bar/Arepera Chaplin** (Wp.24 205M).

The **PR19** is ostensibly a tour of the springs dotted about the hillside behind **Breña Alta**, but the real star of the show is the magnificent chestnut forest. Water is available en route, but take your own, too. The itinerary is well waymarked and signposted.

*in **San Pedro**

Access: by car
Park at Wp.2

Access by bus:
N°s L1 or L91.

Short Versions
To Wp.6 or Wp.9, returning the same way.

We start from the main plaza in **San Pedro** (Wp.1 0M) opposite the post-office bus-stop and, more importantly, the **Bar Teneguia** (see below). Heading south on the main road, we continue on the tarmac when the pavement ends and, 150 metres later, just after a large, pink house, turn right on the access road for the **Viveros Las Breñas**, descending into the **Barranco Aguasencio** (Wp.2 5M) where the **PR19** officially starts.

Climbing past the last houses

Taking the concrete track up the *barranco*, we climb past the **Cerrajeria San Pedro**, where the concrete gives way to tarmac. At a Y-junction (Wp.3 15M) below a house with green gates, we bear left, climbing past the last houses onto a dirt trail. The trail climbs steadily up the *barranco*, passing a first, unnamed *fuente* (Wp.4 25M) before reaching a junction marked by a vandalised PR-signpost (Wp.5 37M). The left-hand fork leads to **Fuente Grande** (Wp.6 40M), which isn't much of a *fuente* (its waters are siphoned off elsewhere), but is a pleasantly shady spot nestling below low cliffs.

For the main walk, we bear right at Wp.5 and climb steeply, passing a vandalised waypost (Wp.7 45M) and gradually bearing south into the heart of the chestnut woods. Crossing a swale beside a ruined cabin, we climb earthen steps and cross a grassy dirt track (Wp.8 55M) onto the path for **El Llanito** - note that this is the signpost direction we follow for the rest of the walk.

Steep dirt steps braced by retaining logs descend to a footbridge, after which we wind round the hillside, gradually descending to **Fuente Espinel** (Wp.9 60M), where there are stone benches and tiny niches chiselled in the rock to frame twig crosses.

Climbing away from the *fuente*, we emerge from the denser woodland into an open area of fern and *brezo*, where we cross in quick succession two dirt tracks (Wp.10 65M) before returning to shady woodland.

This pattern, passing in and out of woodland, is repeated for the next fifty minutes. A few minutes after Wp.10, we re-cross the second dirt track and, twenty-five metres later, at a bend in the dirt track, bear right (SW) on a path descending to a junction (Wp.11 70M). **Fuente Melchora** is ten metres to the right, but we bear sharp left for **El Llanito**, descending to cross a dry watercourse.

Climbing back into the open, we come to a Y-junction next to an electricity pylon, the two branches rejoining some fifty metres later. When the path runs into a dirt track (Wp.12 77M) we maintain direction (SE) for 100 metres, then bear right (W) on another dirt track. The track swings round to the south and climbs gently to another junction (Wp.13 85M) where we take the second branch on the left. The track ends at the **Fuente Aduares** waterpipe (Wp.14 90M) – the *fuente* itself is 75 metres away, shortly after a stone picnic table (no seats!), and is of no great interest unless you need to fill your water bottle.

Crossing the pipe, we take a path which climbs briefly but steeply to a wayposted junction (Wp.15 93M) where we bear left, descending to join yet another dirt track (Wp.16 95M). Turning left, we descend steadily, passing a small cabin on our left, forty metres metres after which we turn right on a PR signposted path (Wp.17 102M).

The shrines

This path climbs, which may seem perverse when we're leaving a track that looks all set for a gentle descent to **San Pedro**, but it's worth it, because as the path doubles back (SW) below a large bluff, it passes two extraordinary little shrines, decked out with flowers (synthetic and real) and dozens of plastic icons.

The path continues to a dirt track (Wp.18 115M), where we bear right. When the track joins a tarmac lane (Wp.19 120M), we turn left and descend to a bend in the **El Pilar** road (Wp.20 130M). Turning left on the alleyway between the road and a yellow-and-green house, we take a side road descending to another bend in the **El Pilar** road (Wp.21 140M), where we bear left again (NNE) on a concrete lane.

Ignoring a private road branching right, we follow the lane as it bears north and runs into tarmac, descending to the main road between **Breña Alta** and **Mazo**, just south of the bridge over the **Barranco de Aduares** (Wp.22 150M).

Rather than following the busy road all the way back to **Breña Alta**, we cross the bridge then, fifty metres later, bear right on the **Camino las Curias**. This pleasant lane leads to the road below the **Viveros** in the **Barranco Aguasencio**, where we turn left to climb back to Wp.2. If you feel like a contrast after this peaceful walk, I strongly recommend the **Bar Teneguia**, a lively working man's café serving great meatballs, chick-peas, stews and the like.

A classic itinerary along the **Cumbre Nueva**, the crest linking the volcanoes of **Cumbre Vieja** and the **Caldera de Taburiente**, preferably done on a clear day the better to appreciate the striking contrast between the lush forests on the eastern flank of the spine and the volcanic wasteland above **Llano de Jable**. Follows the **PR1**, **GR131**, & **PR14**.

| 5 | 4¾ H | 18 km | 675m / 675m | ↻ | 0 |

N.B. If doing the route in reverse, see notes in the text marked **.

Access: by car or bus N° L1

Short Version	Stroll
Taxi to **El Pilar** and follow the walk in reverse to the **Centro de Visitantes**.	From **El Pilar** along the *pista*.

Taking the main track at 25 minutes

Starting just west of the **El Pilar Centro de Visitantes**, where there's ample parking and a bus-stop, we follow **Calle Calderón** (Wp.1 0M N) to a crossroads (Wp.2 10M), where we turn right on the **PR1** to **Virgen del Pino**. A gentle then steady climb leads to the *ermita*, behind which two dirt tracks climb into the woods.

Ignoring the fainter track to the left and a path branching right, we take the main track for 'Cumbre Nueva/Santa Cruz' (Wp.3 25M).

The track is soon obscured by a dense blanket of pine needles, but ignoring all branches and staying to the right of a long, tumbledown wall, we climb steadily along a wooded spur (ENE), till we come to a paved donkey trail (Wp.4 45M), sometimes known as the **Camino del Reventón**. Zigzagging up the paved trail, we climb above the woods to barer, rockier terrain where the spur narrows and steepens, and the switchbacks get tighter.

The views improve the higher we go, until a long straight stretch brings us to the final couple of switchbacks, and we emerge on the **Pista Hilera de la Cumbre** (Wp.5 100M), beside a small *fuente* and in front of a long stone bench overlooking **Santa Cruz**.

N.B. If doing this in reverse, the *ermita* turning is signposted, and comes just before a Y-junction of dirt tracks, the branch to the left signposted 'Pico de la Nieve', the branch to the right 'GR131 Roque de los Muchachos'.

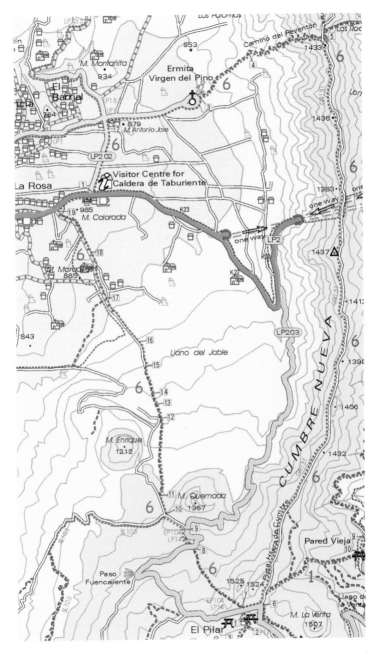

Turning right, we follow the **GR131** along the dirt track (S), all the way to the **El Pilar** road, passing several antennae after half-an-hour. After forty-five minutes, we can see to the west, at the head of a long grey lava flow, two small volcanoes.

... fine views of Birigoyo ...

The higher, broken crater is **Montaña Quemada**, the better formed smaller crater **Montaña de Enrique**. Our return route passes between these two volcanoes. The track gets rather dusty and monotonous toward the end, but fine views of **Birigoyo** (see Walk 7) compensate in the final stretches before the road (Wp.6 180M).

Bearing right, we follow the road down to the **El Pilar Área Recreativa/Zona de Acampada**, where a signpost indicates the 'PR14 Llanos del Jable / El Paso / Tacante' (Wp.7 183M). Forty metres further down the road, we bear right through a gap in the *zona de acampada* fence, bringing us round to the left of the 'sentry-box' shower cabins, perched over a shallow watercourse. We cross the camping area running parallel to the watercourse until, at the NW corner, ten metres from the end of the fence, the watercourse flattens out and feeds into a yellow-and-white PR-waymarked path.

The path, faint at first, soon becomes clearer as it tunnels through the woods, emerging in a gully alongside a huge bank of *picon* before descending to cross the road (Wp.8 200M). Crunching coarse *picon* underfoot, we descend to a bend in the road, where we bear left (Wp.9 205M) on a broad track across the bleak, exposed slopes behind **Montaña Quemada**. At a wayposted Y-junction (Wp.10 210M), we bear right towards the small wooded **Montaña de Enrique**, and then right again at the next Y-junction (Wp.11 215M).

After a steady descent, we reach a bend in a major dirt track (Wp.12 227M), where we bear right on a broad trail, descending to cross another dirt track (Wp.13 230M) which we rejoin thirty metres lower down. Bearing left, we follow the dirt track and, just after it runs into a tarmac lane, turn right to recover the broad trail (Wp.14 232M). The trail widens to a dirt track, first crossing the lane (Wp.15 240M) then joining it at a junction with a track for **La Montañeta** (Wp.16 245M).

Following the lane down to a Y-junction (Wp.17 255M), we bear left on a dirt track cutting out a loop in the lane. Ignoring a red-waymarked branch to the west, we follow this track (N) until it rejoins the lane (Wp.18 265M), which we stick to all the way to the main road (Wp.19 275M).

N.B. If doing this itinerary in reverse, the lane is called **Calle La Moraditas. Bearing right, we follow the main road back to our starting point.

Pico Birigoyo is the northernmost of the high volcanic peaks along the **Cumbre Vieja** and an ideal introduction to the famous **Ruta de los Volcanos**. It's a relatively easy walk, but gets a 4 rating for exertion due to the rough paths at the top and the steep descent. The fact that someone has scrawled 'Ouf!' on the signpost at Wp.5 was not taken into consideration. Not recommended when there's poor visibility or a strong wind. The signposted ascent from **Pista de Llanos de la Mosca** is not recommended. Walking boots essential - anyone wearing sports shoes will end up with a footfull of grit.

Access: by car/TF. Park opposite the huge *Área Recreativa* at **El Pilar**.

Extension
If arriving by taxi, see Walk 6 Wp.7+ for the descent

From the **El Pilar** parking area (Wp.1 0M), we take the **GR131** for 'Los Canarios', crossing the *área recreativa* and passing the main administrative building, beyond which the **Ruta de los Volcanos** begins (Wp.2 3M). Following a broad path through the pine, we climb steadily, zigzagging up to a junction (Wp.3 15M), where we turn sharp right to continue on the GR

The path gradually emerges from the tree cover with fine views to the north, passing an orientation picture board (Wp.4 20M). The pines are more widely scattered as we climb alongside the base of **Birigoyo**, and get our first glimpse of *picón*, the grey volcanic grit that covers the **Cumbre Vieja**. Approaching

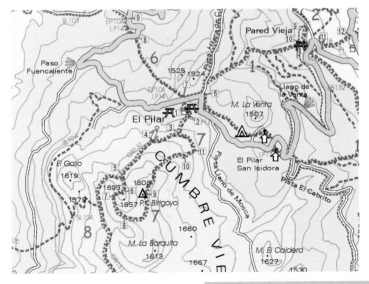

what appears to be a small, discrete cone, we leave the GR on a path signposted 'Birigoyo' (Wp.5 30M).

Approaching the summit

This slippery, gritty path climbs steeply, splintering at the top before emerging on a breach in the **Volcán de San Juan** (Wp.6 40M). Turning right, we climb a faint cairn-marked way over rocks studded with pink houseleeks. When the path levels out (Wp.7 50M), we ignore several parallel paths lower down, and stay near the rim. Passing a small windbreak (Wp.8 55M), we gradually circle the crater till we're heading due north on a broad clear path leading to the **Pico Birigoyo** trig point (Wp.9 70M), from where we have superb views through 360 degrees.

To descend, we take the clear path snaking away toward the **Pista Hilera de la Cumbre** (NE). Descending through *picón* isn't so much a walk as a controlled skid and we rapidly skitter down this steep path, skirting a partial crater before recovering the shade of the pine (Wp.10 85M).

Pista Hilera de la Cumbre

Our narrow path now winds through and along the edge of the pine forest before switching back across the head of a broad firebreak (Wp.11 90M). Once we've re-crossed the firebreak, we follow the path through the heart of the woods (NW), maintaining direction when we join another minor path, just thirty metres from our outward route at Wp.3.

8 RUTA DE LOS VOLCANOS

Of all the walks in La Palma, this is The Big One that ramblers feel they *have to* do - understandably, as nature, with a little help from humankind, has forged a perfect day-hike following the stunning line of volcanoes strung along the **Cumbre Vieja** like so many humps on some fantastical sea monster. The route is strenuous, but not as mammoth as its reputation; expecting to take six hours, I finished in five, breaks included - bear this in mind, I may have had an uncommonly quick day!

In keeping with our policy of sticking to waymarked routes, the described itinerary follows the **GR131**, which studiously avoids some of the more spectacular rim sections of the traditional route - variations can be concocted using Walks 7&9, while a more adventurous Over The Top alternative is indicated in the text. A lot of work has been done on the path, until 1920 the main land link between **Fuencaliente** and **Santa Cruz**, and it's rarely rough underfoot, but good boots are still advisable. It's well waymarked and regularly signposted (though they seem to have run out of posts slotted to indicate corners, resulting in some peculiar configurations with the path) and, as described, poses no problems of vertigo. Wind and mist can be a problem, but even if **El Pilar** is under cloud, the crest may be clear. It's generally fresh on top, even in summer, but the sun is intense, and the descent to **Fuencaliente** (signposted 'Los Canarios') can be infernal.

*in Fuencaliente. The **Bar/Restaurante Centauria** serves good, fresh *tapas* and the excellent **Patio del Vino** provides slightly more sophisticated cuisine.

Extensions
See Walks 7&9 and Wps. 6&11

Access: taxi to **El Pilar**, then bus N° L3 from **Fuencaliente**

Following Walk 7 to Wp.5 (30M), we ignore the **Birigoyo** path and continue on the **GR131** (WSW) which descends slightly to join a broad dirt track (Wp.6 40M) and the **SL104** from **El Paso** (the **SL105** link with Walk 11 joins the track a little way to the north; both are alternative ways onto the present itinerary for the cash-strapped and/or taxi-phobic). Maintaining a southerly bearing, we climb steadily up the track, ignoring several branch paths on the left and one track to the right.

As the track bears east for **Birigoyo**, we branch right (SE) on a broad trail (Wp.7 55M) signposted 'Los Canarios'. Winding through the pine, we climb very slightly, possibly wondering where all the volcanoes are, the only evidence so far being the debris scattered between the trees. Our first clue comes as the pine become more sparse and a couple of small conical peaks appear to the east. After climbing a small rise, we descend slightly in sight of the superbly mottled head of the **Barranco de Tamanca**. A long level stretch skirts **Montaña de los Charcos**, before the path swings sharp left and climbs to cross a footbridge over a gully (Wp.8 75M).

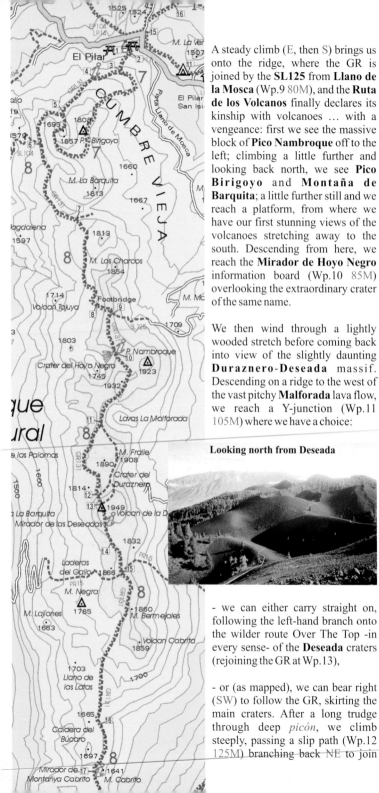

A steady climb (E, then S) brings us onto the ridge, where the GR is joined by the **SL125** from **Llano de la Mosca** (Wp.9 80M), and the **Ruta de los Volcanos** finally declares its kinship with volcanoes … with a vengeance: first we see the massive block of **Pico Nambroque** off to the left; climbing a little further and looking back north, we see **Pico Birigoyo** and **Montaña de Barquita**; a little further still and we reach a platform, from where we have our first stunning views of the volcanoes stretching away to the south. Descending from here, we reach the **Mirador de Hoyo Negro** information board (Wp.10 85M) overlooking the extraordinary crater of the same name.

We then wind through a lightly wooded stretch before coming back into view of the slightly daunting **Duraznero-Deseada** massif. Descending on a ridge to the west of the vast pitchy **Malforada** lava flow, we reach a Y-junction (Wp.11 105M) where we have a choice:

Looking north from Deseada

- we can either carry straight on, following the left-hand branch onto the wilder route Over The Top -in every sense- of the **Deseada** craters (rejoining the GR at Wp.13),

- or (as mapped), we can bear right (SW) to follow the GR, skirting the main craters. After a long trudge through deep *picón*, we climb steeply, passing a slip path (Wp.12 125M) branching back NE to join the Over The Top route. At a second slip path, we double back a few metres to the **Deseada** trig point (Wp.13 130M), the highest elevation on the walk.

Continuing south, we pass the **Mirador de las Deseadas** information-board listing recent eruptions, and descend steeply on a slippery path to the first skew-whiff signpost (Wp.14 135M). Continuing along the ridge, we cross the **PR15** between **Jedey** and **Tigalate** (Wp.15 140M), and bear slightly left (SE), climbing briefly before dipping down and traversing a gritty hollow into a long shallow valley behind the wooded slopes of **Montaña El Cabrito**.

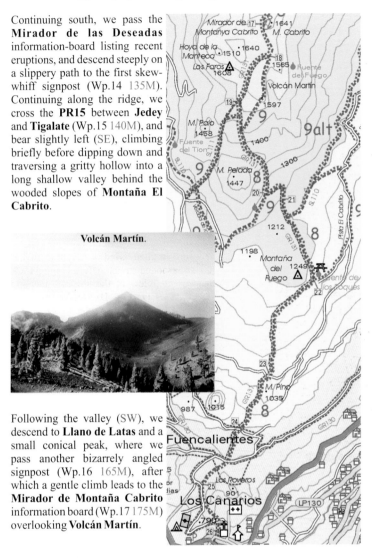

Volcán Martín.

Following the valley (SW), we descend to **Llano de Latas** and a small conical peak, where we pass another bizarrely angled signpost (Wp.16 165M), after which a gentle climb leads to the **Mirador de Montaña Cabrito** information board (Wp.17 175M) overlooking **Volcán Martín**.

Descending to a Y-junction north of **Volcán Martín** (Wp.18 180M), we bear right (see Walk 9 for the crater branch). Skirting to the west of the volcano, we pass three branch paths down to the **SL111**, the third of which is signposted (Wp.19 185M). The GR then descends to the east of **Montaña Pelada's** twin peaks, passing another peculiarly aligned signpost, soon after which we veer sharp left (Wp.20 200M) to descend steeply then steadily east. At successive signposts, we bear right to resume our southerly direction then, a couple of minutes later, left (Wp.21 205M), leaving the broad trail and taking a narrower path channelled by low stone walls.

After crossing the **SL110 Vereda de las Cabras**, we skirt to the east of **Montaña del Fuego**, passing a signposted turning on our left down to 'Fuente Los Roques' (Wp.22 215M) an *área recreativa* with water, picnic tables and barbecues, and in an emergency a forest guard with a walkie-talkie, but <u>not</u> a refuge as the symbol on the sign suggests. The GR circles behind **Montaña del Fuego**, passing another signpost that cheerfully contradicts the obvious, waymarked route descending toward the antenna-topped **Montaña del Pino**. After a long, steady descent through young pine, we cross the dirt track (Wp.23 230M) linking the **Pistas del Oeste** and **Este** (the tracks flanking the **Cumbre Vieja**) and curve to the west of **Montaña del Pino**, crossing another dirt track and bearing left (the signpost gets it wrong again!) on a broad trail that initially runs parallel to the track.

The trail narrows, descending gently between 'kerb' stones to a rougher, slightly steeper stretch, after which low walls define the clear path we follow nearly all the way to **Fuencaliente**. After crossing the **Fuencaliente** dirt track (Wp.24 240M), the walled path intersects with the **GR130** and crosses the track again. At the third junction with the track (Wp.25 250M), we bear left and follow the track. Shortly after a branch on the right down to the football field (which doubles as a campsite), we leave the dirt track, bearing left on a signposted path that brings us within sight of **Fuencaliente**.

Crossing the dirt track for the last time, we descend past the tennis courts to the church (Wp.26 70M) from where we stroll down to the main road for refreshment, transport and accommodation.

Compared to the lush foliage of the north, the south can seem excessively austere, but once you get up in the mountains, what looks bleak from below becomes a fascinating puzzle of delicately shaded rock and deep craters crammed together like a crumpled honeycomb. Using the tail end of the traditional **Ruta de los Volcanos**, the new route followed by the **GR131**, and two *senderos locales*, this circuit provides an excellent introduction to the region. In summer, start early to avoid the midday heat.

For **Short Versions** see end of this walk description.

Access: by car

From **Montes de Luna**, 3.4km south of **Montes de Luna** *supermercado*, turn sharp right on the track for 'Fuente de los Roques / Pino de la Virgen', resetting the odometer at zero. Turn left at km 3.3 on a dirt track signposted (high on a tree to your left) 'Monte del Pino / RTVE / Llano de los Cestos / El Paso', setting the odometer at zero again. Ignore branches on the left for 'Montaña del Pino' and 'Fuencaliente', and bear right at the Y-junction at km 3.1. Park 500 metres later at another junction where our path climbs between the two branches of the dirt track, signposted 'Fuente del Tión / A la Vereda de las Cabras'.

From **Fuencaliente**, turn left fifteen metres north of the **CEPSA** petrol station at the brightly painted green and yellow house. Three hundred metres later, turn right, then left after 100 metres onto a dirt track, setting the odometer at zero. Ignoring branches down to the football field, bear right at the Y-junction at km 1.4, left at km 2.3, and right at km 6.2. The walk starts at km 6.7.

The start of the route

From the junction of dirt tracks (Wp.1 0M), our path climbs steeply then steadily to cross the **SL110 Vereda de las Cabras** (Wp.2 10M), signposted 'Ruta de los Molinos' to the right, 'Fuente del Tión 'to the left. We maintain direction (NE) on the **SL111**, trudging steadily up a long, broad, gritty path behind the western dome of **Montaña Pelada**, gradually bringing **Volcán Martín** into view before emerging on a small rise (Wp.3 40M) within sight of a GR signpost. The **SL111** maintains direction (NE) to join the GR at the signpost, but for a gentler climb, we bear right (ENE) and cross a thin fringe of young pine flanking the GR.

Turning left on the clearly trodden GR (Wp.4 43M), we pass the official junction with the SL (Wp.5 50M) and climb through *picón* to a broad col (Wp.6 60M). Crossing the col, we ignore a minor path to the left and climb to a waypoint (Wp.7 65M), where we leave the GR, turning sharp right onto **Volcán Martín**. At the junction thirty metres later, we bear right, climbing round the rim of the crater to the red, 1597 metre summit at its southern tip (Wp.8 75M).

A controlled skid descent

To descend, we take the boot-churned reddish route to the SW. Using the controlled-skid technique, we skitter down at a hell of a lick (there's no choice about this, but don't build up too much speed as the *picón* is shallower and less skiddable lower down) to rejoin the GR (Wp.9 85M). Breaks aren't normally scheduled, but everyone will have boots full of grit here, so I've allowed a few minutes for pouring out the *picón*.

Bearing left, we follow the **GR131** for a more sedate descent, skirting to the west of the twin peaks of **Montaña Pelada** and passing a GR signpost (Wp.10 90M).

When the GR turns sharp left at a second signpost (Wp.11 95M), we carry straight on for 'Fuente del Tión/Al Vereda de las Cabras' on a clear, rock-lined path winding between pine and passing on our right a small, dry *fuente* (Wp.12 98M). After a gentle descent, gradually curving round to the west, we cross a dirt track (Wp.13 105M) and join the **Vereda de las Cabras**. Continuing in the direction of 'Fuente del Tión/Pista del Oeste' (WNW), we cross the minor track climbing from our starting point (Wp.14 15M) and rejoin our outward route at Wp.2, where we turn left to return to the car.

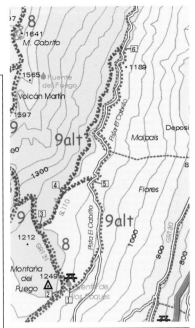

Short Versions
(9 alt) Under The Volcano

Not necessarily 'shorter' but considerably easier, traversing the extraordinary lava-scape below **Volcán Martín**.

2 walker, 55 or 125 minutes, 7.5 kilometres, ascents & descents 100 metres

Access: by car

Take the 'Fuente de los Roques/ Pino de la Virgen' dirt track, but ignore all branch tracks and follow the signs for 'Fuente de los Roques', 5.2km from the road.

From inside the **Fuente de los Roques Área Recreativa** (Wp.1 0M), take the **Monte del Fuego** path up to the **GR131** (Wp.2 10M). Turn right for **El Pilar** and right again at the junction with the **SL110 Vereda de las Cabras** (Wp.3 25M). After crossing a moonscape of jagged black lava, the green-and-white waymarked *vereda* swings sharp right (Wp.4 35M) between two large cairns.

Either turn right to follow the *vereda* down to the **Pista El Cabrito** (Wp.5 40M) or continue straight ahead (NE), on a narrower path marked with smaller cairns that winds through the woods to join the *pista* further along (Wp.6 80M). In either case, return along the **Pista El Cabrito** to the *área recreativa*, fifteen minutes from Wp.5, thirty-five minutes from Wp.6.

San Antonio and **Teneguía** are La Palma's best known volcanoes, largely thanks to accessibility and the fact that **Teneguía** erupted in 1971. The paths are not the most interesting the island has to offer, but there's a grand controlled-skid down from **San Antonio**, and the views are superb. There's a slight risk of vertigo on **Teneguía**, which can be dangerous when the wind's strong. Whether you climb **Teneguía** at the start or end of the walk is a matter of personal preference. Do it first and you're more likely to have the place for yourself, last and you've saved the most spectacular bit for the end.

* +20M for Teneguía ** **San Antonio**, 5 counting **Fuencaliente** (see Walk 8)

Extension	Strolls
Faro de Fuencaliente and **Playa Echentive** (see description at end of main walk)	San Antonio from Wp.5, **Teneguía** from Wp.1

Access by car or (starting from **Fuencaliente**) **by bus Nº L3**. The walk starts in the **Teneguía** car-park, but can be done top-down (Wp.5+) if you haven't got a car, in which case you may have to pay an entry fee. By car, you can either take the LP-130 for **El Faro**, or the LP-128 towards **Las Indias**. In each case, the **Teneguía** dirt track is signposted. Via the LP-130, set the odometer at zero at the turnoff in **Fuencaliente**, turn right at km 6.6 and left at km 7.9. Via the LP-128, set the odometer at zero at the turnoff in **Fuencaliente**, turn left at km 1.4 and left again at km 3.3, then sharp right at km 5.1.

From the **Teneguía** car-park (Wp.1 0M), we take a minor dirt track to the west. When the track climbs above a large reservoir to the lower **Canal de Fuencaliente** (also known as **Canal del Estado**) (Wp.2 5M), we clamber onto the concrete covered canal and, forty metres further west, bear right on a faint path climbing above the canal to join a broad trail (Wp.3 10M) next to the yellow **Roque Teneguía** (not to be confused with the crater of the same name). A steady climb brings us to the track from the LP-128 (Wp.4 20M) where we join the **GR131**. Turning left, we follow the track till the GR branches right (Wp.5 30M) on a clear gritty path climbing steeply through vineyards. After a long, dusty trudge we emerge above the **San Antonio Bar** (Wp.6 45M) on a large, flat circular area ringed by standing stones.

Bearing right, we follow the western rim of the crater (not particularly colourful but perfectly formed and very large) to the 632 metre trig point (Wp.7 55M), from where we have great views over **Volcán Teneguía** and the coast. Unfortunately, a full circuit of the crater is no longer permitted, so we retrace our steps to the circle of standing stones and bear right, crossing the circle (roughly one o'clock) to a junction of paths (Wp.8 65M) signposted 'Only camels'! Following a rough track (E), we join another better-stabilised track skirting the eastern flank of the crater. Ignoring faint traces to the left, we cross a wasteland of rubble and superficial excavation.

Fifty metres after a metal post on our right and shortly before the track swings left (E), we bear right on a broad, gritty way (Wp.9 70M) descending toward the upper **Canal de Fuencaliente**, which is capped with concrete and clearly visible. Crossing the canal, we see **Teneguía** again, and begin the usual controlled-skid descent through *picón*. After emptying our boots beside the vineyards at the bottom, we descend to the main track from the LP-130 (Wp.10 85M) and turn right, bearing left fifty metres later to return to Wp.1.

Ascending Teneguía

You may think there's no point climbing **Teneguía** having had a superior perspective from **San Antonio**, but it's worth it because the views are even better, including the shattered rim of the crater and the tormented, fractured lava flows to the east. From Wp.1 (0M) we take the obvious, but

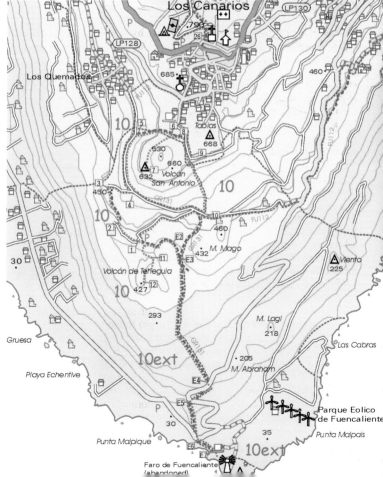

very rough path (SW) towards the northern wall of the volcano, ignoring branches to left (the **GR131**) and right.

At the Y-junction at the start of the climb (Wp.11 5M), we bear right. After crossing a narrow, exposed ridge, we climb steeply and skirt an outcrop of reddish rock, after which a narrow stretch may give vertigo sufferers some qualms. Beyond this, it's an easy stroll round to the small pyramid of rocks at the 427 metre top (Wp.12 10M).

Extension
Faro de Fuencaliente and **Playa de Echentive**

A gentle descent, but a grim ascent in the heat, so only recommended in cool weather or with a pre-arranged taxi at the end.

2 walker (one-way), 4 if climbing back up again, 45 minutes (one-way), descent (& ascent) 400 metres, refreshments: 5

Note: E2 to E7 are map locators, not GPS waypoints.

From Wp.1 (0M) of the main walk, we take the start of the **Teneguía** path, but almost immediately turn left on the clearly waymarked GR. Skirting to the right of a mini-crater, we descend into the valley to the east of **Teneguía**, soon joining a broad dirt trail (E2 7M). Bearing right, we follow the sweep of jagged lava down the valley, bearing right (S) again at a cross-roads of paths (E3 10M) on a narrower but clearly defined path channelled through the volcanic debris.

The lava gradually gives way to finer *picón* and we descend steadily through a lunar landscape to the road (E4 25M), where we bear right. Seventy-five metres later, we turn sharp left to recover the path, partially cutting out a long U-bend in the road. We then cross the road twice more, (E5 & 6 30M & 35M) before coming to the end of the GR at a mapboard (E7 40M) just above the lighthouse and fishing hamlet, where there's a popular fish restaurant.

If you haven't time, transport or inclination to climb higher, yet want to see the mess a volcano can make, the **PR14.1** is the path for you, touring the lava flows (*coladas*) from the **San Juan** volcano, which last erupted in 1949, leaving the **Laderas de Gallo** above **San Nicolás** littered with debris. The route is well waymarked and signposted, and relatively short, but not to be undertaken lightly: the climb is steep, the descent very steep, and the path frequently rough.

	Extensions
Access: by car and bus N° L3	See Wps. 12/13/15 for the **SL103** to **El Pilar** & **El Paso**, the **SL105** to **Cumbre Vieja** (see Walks 7&8), and the **SL106/107** to **Hoyo de la Sima**.

We start from the small car-park between **Bar Americano** and **Bar San Nicolás**, opposite the southbound bus-stop in **San Nicolás** (Wp.1 0M). Heading north along the *carretera general*, we bear right on the LP-117 for **Tacande** and, 200 metres later, just after the football field, right again on a PR-signposted dirt track (Wp.2 5M) climbing through volcanic debris. The track, which is partially asphalted, climbs through a bleak, black landscape relieved only by a small terraced vineyard, after the entrance of which (Wp.3 10M), it dwindles to a steep donkey trail that we follow for the next half-hour.

At first the trail is partially paved, but the man-made paving soon gives way to a carpet of lava. Crossing a rough dirt track (Wp.4 20M), we continue climbing steeply past abandoned terraces and scattered pine. The gradient then eases from steep to steady and we cross a narrow, overgrown path (Wp.5 40M), after which we climb gently on a narrower path, maintaining an easterly direction. The lava-paving becomes more slab-like and grainy, then gradually gives way to gritty dirt.

Joining a rough *picón* and cinder dirt track (chained off to our right), we maintain direction to join another better stabilised track (Wp.6 45M), where we turn left, heading north briefly before turning sharp right on another, broader track (Wp.7 50M). This track climbs gently through an infinitely lazy zigzag before coming to a Y-junction (Wp.8 60M), where we take the roughly paved section to the left. The track then widens and swings north, at which point we bear right on a minor track (Wp.9 65M), passing low cliffs of yellow substrata covered by black rock studded with houseleeks. As the track swings left, we bear right to climb a narrow volcanic channel, cutting out a bend before <u>crossing</u> the same track a few metres later (Wp.10 70M). If you catch a whiff of sulphur round here, don't be alarmed: its source is agricultural rather than satanic or volcanic.

Climbing steeply again, we snake our way up a rocky gully (ESE) on a path that is obscure at first but gradually becomes clearer. Re-crossing the dirt

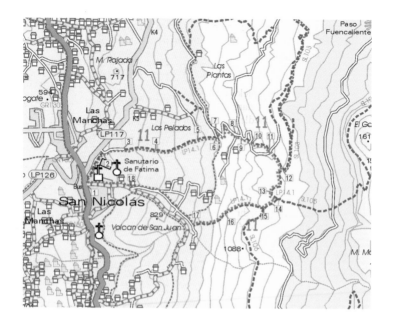

track (Wp.11 80M), we climb steadily to the top of the gully and a signposted junction with the **SL103** to 'El Pilar' and 'El Paso' (Wp.12 90M), where we bear right, sticking to the **PR14.1** as it meanders through blackened pine to an immense field of lava.

The lava field path

Following the signposted path (and it is a path, though lord knows how they made it) we crunch across pumice stones fragilely colonised by lichen and the odd resolute shrub. Passing a signpost for 'Llano de Tamanca', we traverse a flow of lava that looks like it's still molten (Wp.13 100M) and cross a gully, after which we come to a junction with the **SL105** to the 'Pista Forestal Principal' (also known as the **Pista del Oeste**), an alternative way up to the **Ruta de los Volcanos** (see Walk 8). We bear right here, still on the PR, to leave the lava flow and return to a woodland path (Wp.14 105M).

The path soon joins a minor forestry track, where we bear right, striding along on a bed of pine needles that are pleasantly spongy after the sharp volcanic rock. Enjoy them while you can, because they soon become a liability! At the next junction (Wp.15 110M), the track continues (SW) as the **SL106** to 'Llano de los Roques', but we bear right for **Llano de Tamanca**, following a broad way, marked with bright blue waymarks as well as the yellow-and-white we've been following so far. The broad way is obscured by pine needles, but descending (NNW) we soon come to a narrow, clearer path. Unfortunately, it's also very, very steep and carpeted by slippery pine needles that make the descent somewhat precarious.

The bottom of the steep descent

Carefully, very carefully, picking our way down this path (it's not dangerous, but dignity must be maintained!), we cross an ancient terracing wall (Wp.16 125M), after which the gradient is slightly less aggressive. Surfaced with loose dirt and *picón*, the path winds down (unfortunately winding so much the controlled-skid method is nearly all control and very little skid) through mixed pine, almond and wild vine. After passing a small stand of chestnut, we emerge into an open area of scrub and prickly pear, where the path becomes firmer underfoot.

We then squeeze through an overgrown stretch and pass under a palm tree for the final descent between terraces of vines to a dirt track (Wp.17 145M), just above a narrow tarmac lane that was visible through much of the steep descent.

Leaving the **PR14.1**, we bear right on the **SL107**, strolling along the lane (NNW) for a couple of minutes till it swings right and we bear left on a roughly paved track. We stick to this track, maintaining direction when a wider branch swings left to a new house, until we pass two new water tanks and join a tarmac lane (Wp.18 160M), which we follow back to our starting point. The bars in **San Nicolás** are good for a drink, but for a real eating experience, head south for 700 metres on the *carretera general* to the troglodytic restaurant, **Bodegón Tamanca**: a bit of a factory, but the food is very good and the setting extraordinary.

A very short walk that earns its itinerary number for the cliff path down to **Puerto Tazacorte**, a modern, pleasantly laid-back resort that has been developed with a degree of discretion (low-rise, multicoloured, not entirely uniform blocks of flats). It's also the only walk in the book that ends, subject to the usual reservations, with a swim. The route is reasonably well signposted (it's part of the **GR131**), but beware of 'swivelling' waypoints (see Wp.3). There's a slight risk of vertigo.

50 M   3.5 km   600m   N   one way   4

Access: by bus N°s L5 & L2

The start of the route

We start immediately north of the *mirador* bar and souvenir shop, on a rough lane (Wp.1 0M) that descends steeply, swinging round to the west of the *mirador* and passing several branch tracks.

After a steady to steep descent with fine views along the coast towards **Puerto Naos** and inland towards **Cumbre Nueva**, the lane passes between the perforated walls of a banana plantation, and becomes a dirt track (Wp.2 10M).

Crossing a small canal, we bear right on a rough track leading to another lane, where we turn left, descending between banana hothouses, which may have some agricultural interest, but zero aesthetic value, while the shabby open plantations that follow are only marginally better – but don't despair, the best is yet to come! At a T-junction, we turn left, passing the grounds of house N°13. Just after house N°15, we (probably) ignore a signpost (propped between breeze-blocks it's prone to twisting), and turn left on a broad path (Wp.3 20M) that's concreted for the first few metres before running into degraded boulder paving.

After a brief but steady descent between an orchard and a banana plantation, we cross the end of a tarmac road in front of a **Unipalma** warehouse, and recover the roughly paved path, now an authentic donkey trail, bringing us into view of **Tazacorte** beach, which looks completely inaccessible. However, the trail soon passes a rock etched with 'El Bine 250m', after which it doubles back (SE) and begins its dramatic descent down the cliff face to **Puerto Tazacorte**.

Switching back and forth, we descend rapidly, coming onto a 100 metre stretch of dirt (Wp.4 30M) interspersed with occasional patches of paving. After a second, longish, easterly stretch on dirt, the paved and dirt sections alternate. We then pass the first of several small caves (Wp.5 40M) that become increasingly domestic the further we descend, the last one actually being inhabited and equipped with a washing machine, TV and other mod-cons.

Puerto Tazacorte

Shortly after the equipped cave, we emerge on the esplanade between the **Kiosco Teneguía** and, the only old building in the port, the **Restaurante Taberna del Puerto** (Wp.6 45M). One hundred metres along the promenade, we turn left into **Calle Esplanada** and circle behind the modernist sunken plaza.

Crossing the road into the shelter of two fine Indian laurel trees, we bear right for the **Casa del Mar** bus-stop (Wp.7 50M).

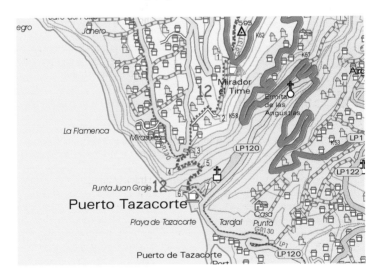

This attractive stretch of the **GR130 is** a good introduction to the domestic landscape and ravines of the north-west. Happily it's littered with signposts, since it criss-crosses such a tangle of tarmac lanes, concrete and dirt tracks, paved trails, cobbled and dirt paths, it reads like a complicated wiring diagram. In view of this, I suggest familiarising yourself with the text beforehand and following the waymarking on the ground, only referring to the book when in difficulty. Traditionally the itinerary ends at **Tijarafe**, but I've extended it to include the spectacular **Barranco del Jorado** (also spelled **Jurado**), a protected area and nesting ground for rooks, kestrels and rock-doves. There's a circuit to be done round this ravine, the **PR12.2**, crossing the bottom of the *barranco* and visiting **Cueva de Candelaria**, but it involves a 650 metre climb – at the end of the walk! Car drivers can descend the northern flank of the *barranco* on concrete and tarmac, but get your nerves galvanised first. The drive scared the living daylights out of us.

Access: by bus N° L5

Stroll	Wps.14-21

The cobbled trail

From the bus-stop in front of **Bar/Restaurante Tinizara** (Wp.1 0M), we follow the road north for 50 metres and then turn left on a tarmac lane. Descending past a chapel and the **Vino Tendal** retail outlet, we branch right after house N°20 on a partially cobbled trail (Wp.2 9M), re-crossing the lane fifty metres later.

We now descend steadily (WSW) then steeply into the **Barranco de la Baranda** (literally 'handrail', which maybe wishful thinking as there's nothing very banister like about it). Crossing the bed of the ravine (Wp.3 20M), our trail climbs to pass a small *mirador* with benches, after which it levels off briefly before descending to cross another lane (Wp.4 25M).

The trail dwindles to an intermittently paved path, winding between abandoned terraces dotted with pine, lichen frosted almond, and prickly pear, before descending to rejoin the lane (Wp.5 30M). Turning left, we follow the lane for fifty metres then bear right on a dirt path supported by a recently restored retaining wall, crossing a shallow gully before rejoining the lane. Shortly after the first house on the left, we branch left on another shortcut path, passing house N°9B before rejoining the lane yet again. When the tarmac turns to concrete, we branch right (Wp.6 40M), recovering the paved trail as it traverses another of the numerous nameless *barrancos* along this coast.

A brief climb brings us onto another tarmac lane, where we bear right. The lane soon runs into a dirt track (Wp.7 45M), from where we get our first glimpse of **Tijarafe**. When the dirt track swings left on a concreted stretch climbing to a tarmac lane, we bear right (Wp.8 50M), recovering the paved trail. Passing a small avocado plantation, we join a tarmac driveway, which leads us back (yet again!) to the tarmac lane. Bearing right, we follow the lane till it passes a large green house, immediately after which, we bear left (Wp.9 55M) on a dirt path running below the balcony of house N°13.

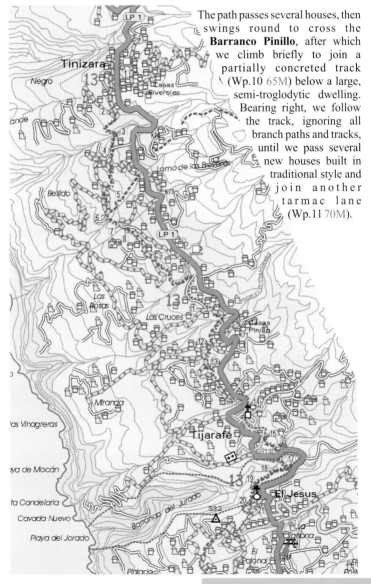

The path passes several houses, then swings round to cross the **Barranco Pinillo**, after which we climb briefly to join a partially concreted track (Wp.10 65M) below a large, semi-troglodytic dwelling. Bearing right, we follow the track, ignoring all branch paths and tracks, until we pass several new houses built in traditional style and join another tarmac lane (Wp.11 70M).

Turning left, we follow the lane to house No. 6 where we take the signposted dirt track to the right. This broad track descends below recently rebuilt terraces into the **Barranco de Cueva Grande**, though the *cueva* isn't that *grande*, so you may prefer to call it by its other name, **Barranco Caldereta**, which can be translated as 'little cauldron' or 'lamb stew'! Bearing right below the *cueva*, we leave the track and take a dirt path, which leads to yet another tarmac lane (Wp.12 80M). Crossing the lane, we briefly recover the paved trail before it disappears in tarmac again! Turning left, we climb along the tarmac lane for a little over 100 metres then, opposite a branch lane on the right (the **PR12.2**), turn left (Wp.13 85M) on a cobbled path climbing to a paved track. Turning right, we soon (inevitably!) rejoin the tarmac lane, which we follow into the outskirts of **Tijarafe**'s modern residential area.

Maintaining direction (SE) past the playground, minimarket and **Casa de la Cultura**, we reach the main road, where we turn right and cross to the 'fishing-smack' car-park. Taking the first turning on the left, signposted 'Bar La Fuente' (Wp.14 95M), we climb towards the church in **Tijarafe**'s old quarter, where we can either carry straight on into **Tijarafe** to wait for the bus in one of the town's rather charmless bars, or turn left on **Calle El Lomo** to complete the walk.

Ignoring the **Camino El Lomo**, we take the first branch road on the right, leaving the built up area. In front of the green gates of house N°3 and three memorial benches, we bear left on a signposted path (Wp.15 105M). Ignoring a branch to the left, we cross the main road (Wp.16 110M) onto a paved trail into the bed of the **Barranco del Jorado**, where the ravine is divided by a long blade of rock (Wp.17 115M). Descending along the northernmost watercourse, we cross a dull gold waterpipe (Wp.18 118M) and turn left up the southernmost watercourse. Thirty metres later, we branch right on a broad dirt path that climbs under a distressingly friable overhang before crossing a pass with superb views up and down the ravine (Wp.19 122M)

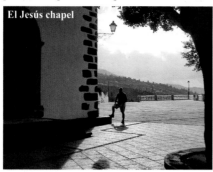
El Jesús chapel

After a steady climb, we emerge on the rim of the *barranco* (Wp.20 130M), where we turn left 'al Sendero Local 71' and climb past the **El Jesús** chapel to the main road (Wp.21 135M). The bus-stop is two hundred metres to the south.

Loosely translated this means 'Cliffs of the Little Tiny Walls', suggesting a strong sense of irony in early hispanic settlers. Following the SL71, we climb from the scattered hamlet of **El Pinar** to the south-western tip of the **Caldera de Taburiente**, and what we get is not 'little tiny walls', but plummeting crags and a birds-eye view of the **Barranco de las Angustias**. Descending via the **GR131** to the **Torre de Time** firewatch tower, we return to **El Pinar** via the **PR10** *traviesa*. If you have no car, either climb from **El Jesús** on the **SL71** (+300 metres), or taxi up to **El Pinar** and, at Wp.12, stay on the **GR131** down to the **Mirador del Time** bar and Walk 12.

Extensions: see itinerary introduction

Access: by car/TF: 200 metres south of the **El Jesús** turn-off (signposted 'Jesús a la Costa') take the tarmac lane climbing east, signposted 'Torre Vig. Inc. de Time', setting the odometer at zero. Ignore all branches (including a green sign indicating **El Pinar** to the right) and park at the start of the **Roque de los Muchachos** dirt track (km 4.8) at the signposted intersection of the **SL71** & **PR10**.

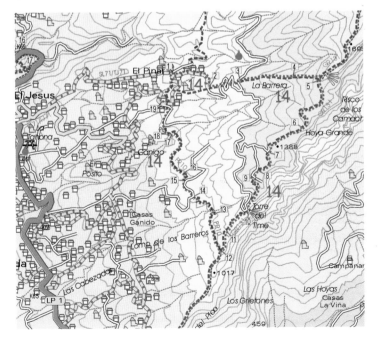

From the parking area (Wp.1 0M) we take the **SL71** (Llano de la Cruz, La Traviesa, Risco de las Pareditas) which climbs steeply up the tarmac lane. The lane dwindles to a newly surfaced concrete track, which we follow till it bears east (Wp.2 10M), at which point we turn left on a broad, rocky trail framed by two cairns. Climbing steeply, as we do throughout the ascent, we cross the concrete track four times, bearing slightly left after the fourth time, away from a short stretch of abandoned forestry track, after which we cross the dirt track (Wp.3 20M) linking **Torre del Time** with the **Refugio Tinizara**, and continue on a route marked by a waypost.

The rest of the ascent, on a broad trail/firebreak, is relatively featureless, hence the infrequent waypoints. There are no branches, but nor is there any variety of landscape as we labour up between badly burned pine. In 2001, a barbecue got knocked over in **Garafía** setting off a conflagration that spread the entire length of the **Caldera de Taburiente**'s western flank. Fire-fighters battled for a week to prevent the flames spilling into the crater itself. The **Garafía** forest is more prone to fires due to the prevailing winds, but the old growth pine that predominate there are more resilient than the young pine further south, which are only now beginning to recover.

At first, the slope is indistinguishable from the surrounding hillsides, but it gradually climbs onto a spur, known as **La Barrera**, defined by two watersheds that ultimately feed into the **Barranco del Jurado**. As the spur narrows so does the trail, dwindling to a path lined with tall thin stones and passing a large charred log in a small pit (Wp.4 50M), after which the path switches back and forth between the northern and southern flanks of the spur, before finally joining the **GR131** (Wp.5 65M). Our onward route bears right for 'Torre del Time/Puerto de Tazacorte', but first, we turn left and climb a few metres to a superb natural *mirador* overlooking the **Barranco de las Angustias**.

Returning to the GR, we descend steadily through blackened pine and the cistus that always spring up after a fire, remaining prudently behind the rim of the crater, until we emerge in the deep hollow known as **Hoya Grande** (Wp.6 80M), overlooking **Llanos de Aridane** and the track into the **Barranco de las Angustias**.

After a long level stretch, the path descends between terraces of vines, the retaining walls studded with enormous houseleeks, then joins the end of a rough dirt track. Immediately after the first bend, we bear left (Wp.7 85M) onto a narrower, more overgrown terrace path, which descends briefly, then levels out and joins another dirt track (Wp.8 90M). We follow this track, passing a branch to the left, fifteen metres after which we bear right (Wp.8 95M) on a broad path descending toward the **Torre del Time** firewatch tower. After crossing a narrow dirt track, we descend onto the main track crossed at Wp.3. Bearing left, we follow this track to the *torre* and **Mirador del Time** (not to be confused with the *mirador* of the same name in Walk 12) (Wp.9 105M).

When the narrow track descending behind the tower swings sharp right, we maintain direction (SW) on a broad rocky trail (Wp.10 110M) down to the signposted junction with the **PR10** (Wp.11 115M), where we turn right onto a narrow path between abandoned terraces. The path dips up and down before winding round to cross a first, unnamed *barranco* choked with ferns (Wp.12 125M). We then pass a very slightly vertiginous stretch before joining the end of a narrow dirt track, which we follow down to a broader dirt track (Wp.13 130M), where we bear right to maintain our northerly direction. After a gentle climb, the track swings sharp right into a second unnamed *barranco* and we turn left onto a waymarked path (Wp.14 135M). The path winds down the flank of the *barranco* before bearing sharp right (E) to cross it, after which a slightly rougher and again, occasionally and very slightly, vertiginous path continues descending (WNW), passing below a large cool cave (Wp.15 140M).

A brief, gentle climb brings us over a small rise, within sight of **El Pinar**, into the triple clefted **Barranco de los Gomeros**. After crossing the three water courses of the *barranco* (the second of which is a shallow watershed), we climb in a westerly direction then, five metres before the first small pine on the right (Wp.16 153M), double back sharp right and climb steeply to a cabin (Wp.17 155M), behind which there's a small reservoir and a line of shady medlar trees. Just above the reservoir, we bear left on a narrow dirt track, crossing another mini-*barranco* before climbing gently to pass behind a cottage with a partially corrugated roof and join the lane through **El Pinar** (Wp.18 160M). Thirty metres up the lane, we bear left on a cobbled path passing between a cottage and outbuildings for a final delightful stroll rejoining the lane just short of Wp.1.

15 CUEVAS DE BURACAS

The **Buracas** caves below **Las Tricias** are popular with organised groups, so you need to get there early if you don't want to be queuing up or crowded off the path (the main guided walks company come here on Tuesdays and Saturdays). Nowadays, the deeper caves have become cosy hideaways for the lucky few and those that remain open are either small or garnished with rubbish, but the paths are still attractive, and the Dragon Trees are among the finest on the island.

* in **Las Tricias Bar/Spar**

Access: by car and bus N° L5

The concrete track

We start on a typically La Palman path going (uncontested!) through everybody's back garden. In front of the **Las Tricias Bar/Spar**, we take a concrete track descending behind the tiny *ayuntamiento* and playground (Wp.1 0M), where we turn left on a cobbled slip path. Following a very narrow dirt path, we skirt a small orchard, at the end of which, we turn right on a concrete lane that ends after fifteen metres at a small house with ceramic name tiles 'AP' (Wp.2 5M).

We continue descending on a narrow path meandering between gardens, small houses, and abandoned fields, until we come to a T-junction with a broad cobbled alley (Wp.3 10M), where we join the **GR130**. Turning right, we follow the alley down to the road, where we turn left, descending past **El Café** and a dental clinic to pass between a bottleneck of old houses, fifty metres after which the road swings right and the GR bears left on a broad cobbled track (Wp.4 20M). We leave both the road and, briefly, the GR, taking the cobbled path between the large white building and the house with a triangle painted on its chimney.

The path broadens to a dirt track leading to a tarmac lane, which we descend, rejoining the GR just above a house where you'll probably be charmingly strong-armed into buying some costly almonds, or even a walking stick if you haven't got your wits about you. Immediately after the house (Wp.5 25M), we turn right on a narrow path that rejoins the lane lower down. Just <u>after</u> the next right-hand bend in the lane (Wp.6 30M), we turn left on an access track then immediately right to recover the old path.

The path descends through an abandoned almond grove, passing the first and largest of the Dragon Trees seen on this itinerary, after which we cross the lane again (Wp.7 35M). Crossing a dirt track a couple of minutes later, we descend past more superb dragon trees to a junction of paths (Wp.8 40M). The GR, which we return on, bears right for **Santo Domingo**, but we continue on the main path, passing a cabin (Wp.9 45M) with a supply line strung across the **Barranco del Corchete**. The path eventually swings right beside a panel advertising orange juice (Wp.10 48M), bringing us into the *barranco*, where we turn right at a T-junction (Wp.11 50M) next to a tiny troglodytic dwelling.

The first Dragon Tree

Crossing the *barranco*, we pass the dry **Fuente de Buracas** (Wp.12 53M), just beyond which are the last open and rather mucky caves. Scrambling up natural rock steps, we follow the GR waymarks, crossing the roof of an 'air-conditioned' cave with an immaculately maintained terrace. After traversing a grove of oranges, lemons, grapes and bananas, we emerge on a dirt track beside a GR waypost (Wp.13 60M), where the trudge back up to **Las Tricias** begins.

Turning right, we start climbing, ignoring a first GR branch to the left and continuing on the track as it runs into tarmac. A steady climb brings us to a second wayposted branch for the GR to 'Santo Domingo' (Wp.14 70M), fifteen metres beyond which, we turn right on a dirt track that ends in a small turning circle behind a house.

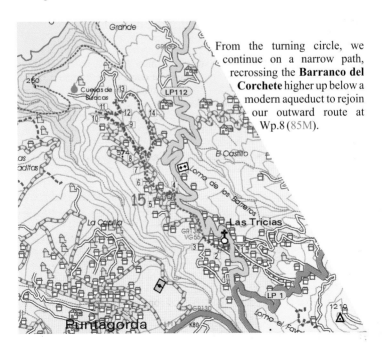

From the turning circle, we continue on a narrow path, recrossing the **Barranco del Corchete** higher up below a modern aqueduct to rejoin our outward route at Wp.8 (85M).

A short itinerary giving an insight into La Palman rural life and introducing the great **Garafía** pine forest. Using the **PR10**, we traverse the heartland of the local livestock industry, passing rough pasture dotted with skeletal broom picked bare by goats, and land stripped of *brezo* and laurel for summer feed when the goats are shut away. We then climb through the fringes of the **Pinar de Garafía Nature Reserve** before descending back through farmland to **El Bailadero** restaurant, a friendly place, pleasantly situated and (rare round here) English speaking. Unfortunately, the food doesn't compare with the local competition (see Walks 18, 19, & 21(a)).

Short Version	Extension
To Wp.5 and back.	Turn left at Wp.5 to join Walk 19, 400 metres down the road.

Access: by car and bus N° L11. Park in the lay-by above **El Bailadero**, a little way north of the junction with the **Roque de los Muchachos** road.

The narrow dirt track

We start just below the restaurant on a narrow dirt track (E) for 'La Mata' (Wp.1 0M). The track soon dwindles to a drovers' trail, dropping into the **Barranco de los Sables**, where it joins another, broader dirt track (Wp.2 5M). Bearing right, we curve behind the bare **Montaña Vaqueros**, passing a major branch to the right (Wp.3 8M), which is our return route.

Maintaining our easterly direction, we ignore all branches and stick to the main track which eventually becomes a tarmac lane (Wp.4 20M). Again ignoring all branches, we follow the lane as it winds through the countryside before climbing to the fringes of the **Garafía** forest, passing a stand of immensely tall pine.

When the lane joins the main road (Wp.5 35M), we turn right, leaving the PR. After 100 metres, just before the next bend in the road, we bear right on a dirt track climbing past a small farm. Climbing steadily through deep, peaceful woods, we pass a grubby, white water-hut, just after which we branch left at a Y-junction (Wp.6 45M). Maintaining our southerly direction and still climbing steadily, we ignore all branches until the track bears right (SW) bringing us to a second Y-junction (Wp.7 55M) where we fork right and right again at a third Y-junction a couple of minutes later.

Our track now winds round the mountainside, with fine views over the farmland round **Montaña Vaqueros**. Immediately after passing a branch to the south, we bear left at a Y-junction (Wp.8 60M) formed by a newly bulldozed branch to the right. We now cross two shallow *barrancos*, the first topped by terraces of vines, the second choked with fern, before climbing to join a track (Wp.9 70M) leading to a house thirty metres above the junction. Maintaining our westerly direction, we follow a grey water pipe above terraced pasture till we reach a T-junction (Wp.10 75M), where we turn right and start descending. Reaching a second T-junction just above a large circular reservoir (Wp.11 80M), we turn left to pass above apple orchards, then bear right on another track a couple of minutes later, rejoining our outward route at Wp.4 (90M).

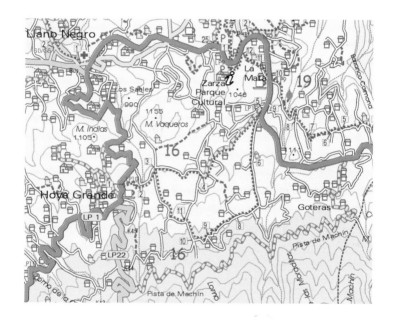

If Robert Mitchum were a town, he'd be **Santo Domingo de Garafía**. It's sleepy, a bit dead and alive, and doesn't seem to be doing very much most of the time, but it does have an undeniable presence and a nonchalant, somnolent charm all of its own. The sort of place to linger and drink up the atmosphere, providing the atmosphere isn't battering you over the head with breathtaking gusts of wind, which it often is. A mix of tidy domesticated landscape and untamed elemental wilderness, our itinerary follows the **SL51**, **PR9**, and **GR130** on bucolic lanes, cobbled donkey trails and sinuous dirt tracks.

Short Version - see text

Access: by bus N°s L5 or L11. The walk starts from bus-stop N°89 between the Red Cross emergency centre and **Llano Negro**, though in future buses will probably stop at the new station on the **Santo Domingo** road, in which case join the walk at Wp.2.

> **Stroll**
>
> Into the **Barranco de la Luz** from **Santo Domingo**

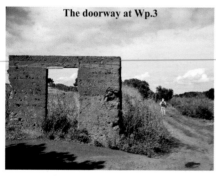

The doorway at Wp.3

From bus-stop N°89 (Wp.1 0M), we stroll through **Llano Negro**, passing the supermarket and a crossroads with an 'SL51' signpost (Wp.2 3M). Maintaining a northerly direction, we descend steeply on a narrow lane leading into open countryside, where we take the second track on the right, next to a doorway, the lone relic of a ruin (Wp.3 8M).

Strolling along the partially cobbled track, we bear right at a Y-junction, after which the track briefly dwindles to a trail. Ignoring two branches on the left leading to small houses, we continue on the track as the semi-agricultural heathland of **Llano Negro** gradually gives way to young pine forest, where we bear right at a second Y-junction. After crossing a dirt track (Wp.5 20M), we continue descending on a narrow donkey trail through mixed heathland and wind-chafed pine.

The trail runs alongside the **Barranco de la Luz**, passing a puzzling PR waymark (I suspect somebody got their pots of paint mixed up!), gradually broadening into an ancient paved cart track. A steep descent, some of it badly eroded, brings us within sight of **Santo Domingo**. Crossing the tip of a concrete track (Wp.6 35M), we continue on the donkey trail before rejoining the track, which we follow for approx. 200 metres. Shortly after passing a car-

port, on our right, and a path to our left, we reach a branch path (Wp.7 40M) doubling back on the right (SE) toward a tarmac lane, behind which there's a large waterpipe.

For the short walk (15M to **Santo Domingo**), we stay on the concrete track (and the **SL51**) which soon runs into an immaculately cobbled section of the lane, the official, signposted junction with the 'PR9'. From here, we simply follow the cobbled cart track alongside the **Barranco de la Luz** into the outskirts of **Santo Domingo**, where we bear right on a tarmac lane down to the green 'tower' block of the main walk (see below).

For the main walk, we turn right at Wp.7, leaving the **SL51**. The path descends to a dirt track, which leads onto the tarmac lane and the **PR9**. We follow the PR along the lane (NE), passing an asphalted branch descending north-west, shortly after which our lane runs into a dirt track (Wp.8 50M) and we leave the PR, turning left on a concrete track signposted 'Casa Turismo Rural Isla Bonita'.

When the concrete ends, we ignore the 'Casa Rural' branch to the left and continue (NE) on the dirt track through a series of unconscionably long switchbacks as it repeatedly approaches then shies away from the nameless *barranco* that descends from the **Casas del Jaral** to the west of the tiny hamlet of **El Palmar**. After a final approach to the *barranco*, at the bottom of which we can see dragon trees and cactus spurge nestling in the folds of the ravine, the track passes a **GR130** signpost (Wp.9 80M) and we turn left for **Santo Domingo** on a broad path alongside a wire mesh fence.

The path, in fact another donkey trail, climbs gently (SW) before crossing a rough dirt track (Wp.10 90M). After a steadier climb, the brightly painted houses of **Santo Domingo** come into view and we first cross then join another track, dirt when we cross it, concrete when we join it, at the end of which (Wp.11 100M), barely a stone's throw from **Santo Domingo**, we are confronted by the dramatic gulf of **Barranco de la Luz**. The concrete ends behind a small house on the edge of the ravine, and we continue on the old paved way, a beautiful trail snaking through the crooked 'M' of the ravine, the walls of which are dotted with caves housing dozens of goats, the cliffs sheltering more dragon trees and spurge.

Santo Domingo, the green 'tower block' visible

A final steep climb brings us into **Santo Domingo** behind a tall green building, the town's token 'tower' block, beyond which we emerge in the main square beside the pleasant **Bar/Cafeteria Plaza** (Wp.12 110M). The bus stop is 200 metres further west, just past the **Bar/Restaurant Taberna Santy**. There are two restaurants in town, neither of them open when we visited.

Two hundred metres west of the bus stop is the **El Bernegal Restaurant**, more upmarket than our usual *tipicos* and stylishly put together; the food is beautifully presented, but not particularly tasty.

There's a touch of the Grand-Old-Duke-of-Yorks about this one: we march down the hill, then we march up the hill, then we turn round and do it all over again! Logical, it ain't, but logic goes out the window on La Palma's northern coast, where walks that are 'logical' in terms of coherence are bonkers when you calculate the accumulated climb.

We start from the village of **El Tablado**, sandwiched between the **Barrancos de Fagundo** and **de los Hombres**, the two biggest ravines in the **Guelguén Nature Reserve**. Despite mass migration (the population is a tenth of what it once was), the village has clung to existence just as it clings to its precarious perch between the ravines, and even boasts an excellent restaurant, **El Moral**. Our route crosses the **Fagundo** on the old coastal path, now part of the **GR130**, linking **El Tablado** with the hamlet of **Don Pedro**, a pleasant enough place, but not really worth the extra 20 minutes and 100 metres once we've crossed the ravine. The pleasure is all in exploring the monumental and otherwise inaccessible **Fagundo**, with its magnificent cliffs, caves to gladden a hermit's heart, and a glut of weird and wonderful cacti.

Don't be deceived by the insignificant little squiggle representing this itinerary on the map. As the crow flies, it's barely a kilometre long, but ramblers aren't crows and this is a strenuous walk. There's a slight risk of vertigo on the western flank of the ravine, otherwise the main hazard is for arachnophobes, the path being criss-crossed by dozens of spiders webs.

Access: by car. The walk starts in the middle of **El Tablado**. Simply follow the concrete lane until you see the 'GR/PR' signpost. There's <u>one</u> parking space beside an abandoned house just below the start. That said, the concrete lane is very narrow and very steep. If your car is big, cumbersome or unfamiliar, you may prefer to park towards the end of the tarmac near the **El Moral** restaurant.

Stroll:
to Wp.2

Short version:
to Wp.3

From the village centre (Wp.1 0M) we take the **GR130** for **Santo Domingo**, a broad path with mock petroglyphs and cave-paintings etched into patches of concrete. After circling to the west of abandoned terraces and passing a couple of dragon trees, we join a paved path descending towards the sea, leaving behind the last house in the village, and descending onto a narrow spur overlooking the *barranco*.

The paved way declines to a rocky path and we enter the **Reserva Natural de Guelguén** (Wp.2 15M). After zigzagging down with great views along the coast beyond **La Fajana**, **El Tablado's** landing when contact with the outside world was by boat, we swing round the spur and enter the *barranco* below patchwork cliffs undermined by shallow caves. Taking care not to slip on the unstable gravel, we descend steeply, passing a tremendous variety of spurge and houseleeks, and one or two deeper caves, before finally reaching the bottom of the *barranco* (Wp.3 30M).

I don't really need to tell you what comes next, as you'll have been looking at it all the way down. Starting our ascent, we pass what must have been an impressive waterfall, and climb round a very slightly vertiginous ledge. The path then levels out above abandoned terraces and below a long, snout-like spur (Wp.4 40M). Winding up the spur, we swing right on another slightly vertiginous stretch, after which a final zigzagging climb out of the *barranco* brings us to a Y-junction (Wp.5 65M).

Bearing left on the broader, rockier path, we climb steadily along the edge of the *barranco*, soon joining a broad trail leading to the first houses of **Don Pedro**, from where we have good views over the affluent feeding the waterfall seen at the start of the ascent (Note: the stone pillar passed just before the houses has no great historical significance, but is a replica of an older one that was destroyed). Just after the second house, we join a dirt track (Wp.6 80M). The **PR9.2** climbs south towards the **Caldera de Agua** and **La Zarza** (see Walks 19&20) while the GR follows the track into **Don Pedro**, a case of 'No Bar, No Go' as far as we're concerned.

We return by the same route and retreat to the **El Moral** restaurant, which specialises in grilled goat's cheese (*queso asado*), pork chops (*chuletas de cerdo*), and whatever happens to be fresh – as the owner said to us, "They don't kill a cow every week"!

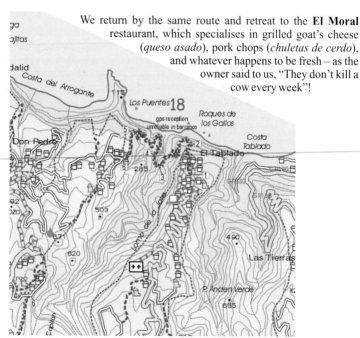

The **Caldera de Agua** isn't marked on most maps; the best places never are! The *caldera* (literally a 'cauldron') is a series of dry waterfalls at the head of the **Barranco de Magdaletín**, hemmed in by the high walls of the ravine and enclosed by a lid of tightly interlacing *laurisilva*. It's a magical place, readily accessible but virtually unknown, and so hushed and tranquil it feels remote. To reach it we cross a succession of ravines fringed with Canary pine, following drovers' trails and parts of the *pista forestal* that, until a decade ago, constituted the main 'road' between the northern villages (one of the old wooden bridges is still visible from the LP1 at the **Barranco Carmona/Cedro** bend, 2.3km east of **La Mata**). And as if that isn't enough, we have the option of a good lunch at the excellent **La Mata** restaurant (closed Wednesdays, the kitchen opens at 1pm, specially recommended are the grilled goats cheese, *queso asado*, marinated goat stew, *cabra con salsa*, and rabbit with garlic, *conejo con ajillo*).

| 3 | 3¾ H | 8.2 km | 300m / 300m | ↻ | 5* |

*also see Walk 21(a)

Access: by car (park on the access road at Wp.1) and bus N° L11: given the bus timetable (dep. **Santa Cruz** 7.10 am, **Barlovento** 8.30 am return shortly after 1 pm) dawdling over the short version, is probably preferable to racing round the full walk.

Short Version	**Stroll**
Start from **La Mata** (Wp.10)	Wps. 12-16

The track at the start of the route

We start from **Roque del Faro**, opposite the second of the hamlet's three access roads, on a broad concrete track signposted 'La Mata/Santo Domingo' (Wp.1 0M). After descending past a large white building, the concrete gives way to dirt carpeted with pine needles. Winding down to traverse a shallow *barranco*, we join another track (Wp.2 5M) and maintain direction (W), crossing a second shallow *barranco* and the **El Tablado** road (Wp.3 15M). Curving round the head of **Barranco Carmona**, the track dwindles to an overgrown path, partially cobbled with large black boulders.

After a short climb on a shady path, we bear right on a grassy track (Wp.4 25M), which turns to deep fine dust as we approach a goat farm. Ignoring a branch to the right, we descend briefly before climbing to a crossroads of dirt tracks (Wp.5 35M). Continuing straight ahead, we climb to a triple fork (Wp.6 38M). Ignoring tracks to left and right, we follow a narrow, grassy path, signposted 'La Mata/Santo Domingo'. After a short, cobbled descent, the

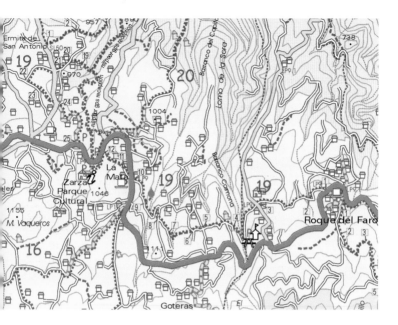

path crosses a deep *barranco* choked with tangled laurel, where it joins another dirt track (Wp.7 40M) and we bear right, climbing above the *barranco*.

We then cross a broader dirt track (Wp.8 45M), part of the old 'road' from the days when the car journey from **Barlovento** to **Garafía** took up to six hours. After a brief descent, we rejoin the 'road' and bear left. We now follow this track all the way to **La Mata**, passing a path down to the 'Fuente del Capitán' (Wp.9 55M) (30 metres below the track and worth a visit, though not a drink), 150 metres after which we reach the LP1 just opposite the **Bar/Restaurante La Mata** (Wp.10 58M).

Crossing the road and the car-park behind the restaurant, we take the track for **San Antonio/Santo Domingo** (Wp.11 60M), which dwindles to a path descending to rejoin the road (Wp.12 65M) 50 metres east of the **Zarza Parque Cultural**. Descending to the small car-park in front of the Visitors' Centre, we turn right through a tunnel under the road, signposted 'PR9.2/9.3 Caldera de Agua/Don Pedro/Santo Domingo'. One hundred metres from the road, just before several caves, we leave the main trail and bear left on an idyllic woodland path following the bed of a dry stream (Wp.13 75M). Joining a broader path (Wp.14 80M), we bear right for 'Don Pedro/Caldera de Agua' and, 25 metres later, left (Wp.15) on a steep, stepped descent into the head of the **Barranco Magdaletín** and the first of three *calderas*. (Note: Waypoints in the *barranco* are not the same as for Walk 20, so don't waste time puzzling over apparently superfluous waypoint symbols on the map.)

Once in the *barranco*, we bear right on another perfect streambed path lined with apple trees. Crossing a wooden footbridge (Wp.16 85M), we climb above then traverse the face of a second, more spectacular *caldera*. A second bridge then re-crosses the watercourse, which plunges away below us as we continue along the right bank. Ignoring a branch path climbing to the right (Wp.17 95M), we descend to the bottom of the heavily wooded *barranco*. Crossing a third bridge (Wp.18 100M) we pass in front of an extraordinary cave set into the base of falls studded with bolted rock handholds. Fifteen metres after the bridge we leave the PR (which continues down the *barranco*) and turn left on a partially cobbled path marked with a red dot. Bearing left at a Y-junction 20 metres later, we climb steeply on a shady path, finally emerging on the level (Wp.19 115M) behind farm buildings, within sight of the antennae-topped **Montaña de San Anton**.

When the path joins the farm track (Wp.20 117M) we bear left and then right at a Y-junction 150 metres later (Wp.21 119M). Crossing the **El Mudo/Juan Adalid** road (though you could turn left here and go directly to Wp.24), we follow a dusty dirt track to a signposted T-junction (Wp.22 125M). Turning left for 'La Zarza/Roque del Faro/Roque de los Muchachos' then bearing left again at a Y-junction (Wp.23 27M), we follow a partially cobbled path back to the **El Mudo** road (Wp.24 130M). Crossing the road, we take the narrow tarmac lane directly ahead of us, which we follow back to the LP1 (Wp.25 140M). **La Zarza** is one hundred metres to the left.

Once you've visited the **Caldera de Agua**, you'll be looking for a pretext to go back. Happily, the local authorities have provided one in this perfect circuit between **La Zarza** and **Don Pedro**. Less happily, half the signposts have been uprooted and the waymarking at the start is a mite abstemious, but don't let that discourage you. The route is straightforward and the full **PR9.2** in the ravine a must-do. (Note that waypoints in the *barranco* are not the same as for Walk 19, so don't waste time puzzling over apparently superfluous waypoint symbols on the map.)

| 4 | 2 H | 7 km | 400m / 400m | ↻ | 5* |

Stroll: (see Walk 19)

* see Walk 19

Access: by car and bus N° L11. Park in the **Parque Cultural La Zarza** overflow car-park on the northern side of the main road, between **La Zarza** and the **Don Pedro** turn-off.

From the car-park (Wp.1 0M), we follow the main road (NE) up past the **Don Pedro** turn-off and bus stop, fifty metres after which we branch left on a narrow tarmac lane (Wp.2 5M). Five metres before the tarmac gives way to dirt we turn right (NE) on a rough dirt track (Wp.3 15M), the fourth on the right after Wp.2.

At the first Y-junction (Wp.4 20M), we fork left (N then NW), passing two branches on the left before veering north-east again. When the track bears west (Wp.5 25M) we maintain direction (NNE) on a narrower, grassier trail that brings us in sight of the sea.

The small shrine at Wp.7

The trail briefly dwindles to an overgrown path before broadening again below an abandoned cabin. Descending a wooded ridge alongside the **Barranco del Capitán** (NNE), we pass a small farmstead where the trail becomes a partially concreted track leading to a tarmac lane (Wp.6 40M). Turning sharp left, we follow this lane till it joins the **Don Pedro** road. The path to **Don Pedro** continues fifty metres down the road, but we bear left and climb to a small walled shrine, directly above which is the broad path (Wp.7 50M) into the **Caldera de Agua**.

Burrowing into the woods with tantalising glimpses of the **Barranco Magdaletín** (N), we pass a small *fuente* with a trough and then a large pool springing from a cleft in the rock (Wp.8 55M). Zigzagging down into the densely wooded ravine, we cross the watercourse five minutes later and start climbing up the *barranco* (S), sometimes on the left bank, sometimes the right, often following the watercourse itself. Tunnelling under a tangle of tall, thin chestnut and laurel, carpeted with dead leaves, lined with large fern and mossy boulders, and scored with birdsong, this path is a sylvan paradise that ought to be as celebrated as the island's better known routes, but is for the present gloriously neglected.

At the first, long, staired section (Wp.9 65M), we climb steps so badly eroded they're little more than a ladder of log stair-rods, before dipping down back into the bed of the *barranco*. Continuing up the bed of the *barranco*, we cross a large outcrop of rock (Wp.10 75M), briefly recovering a path on the left bank. Constantly switching back and forth between left and right banks, often as not imperceptibly, we finally come to a narrow stretch between low cliffs mottled with moss and fringed with creepers, after which we pass a small *fuente*/trough/*lavadero* (Wp.11 85M) and join the route of Walk 19 below the *caldera*/waterfall with a cave at its base.

For a generic description of the remainder of the route, see Walk 19. Crossing the bridge below the first waterfall, we climb steeply on a stepped path (NE) before swinging back to our general southerly direction and passing a large blank mapboard (Wp.12 95M). The path runs alongside the watercourse before crossing a second bridge and traversing the face of the largest of the three waterfalls. Switching back behind the second falls, we cross a third bridge. Emerging from the woods into a broad valley choked with ferns, we pass abandoned apple trees, and stroll along a level path back into shady woodland. The path broadens to a dirt track, which we leave at a Y-junction (Wp.13 105M), bearing right on a waymarked path leading to the third and smallest waterfall.

Turning left in front of the waterfall, we climb to rejoin the dirt track. Bearing right, we follow the track for 25 metres and then branch left on a shady path for **La Zarza**. This delightful sun-dappled path joins another track/trail next to small caves (Wp.14 115M). Bearing right, we pass under the road into the main **La Zarza** car-park, a little way to the west of our starting point.

(a) Barranco de los Hombres

Barranco de los Hombres is one of the largest ravines in the north, an area not notably short of large ravines, but in this gentle stroll, we favour easy walking on the wooded slopes at the head of the *barranco*. What's true of the ravine is true of the *típico*, too. In a region chock-full of fine country restaurants, the **Reyes** is outstanding: menu, cuisine and decor are all very simple, but so is the sense of well-being inspired by their rabbit stew (*conejo con salsa*). Eat in the bar to enjoy the loud bonhomie of local farmers having their midday beer.

Access: by car or bus N° L11. Parking is plentiful around the restaurant. Both itineraries are on or near the bus route, but are more suitable as a break from car-touring.

Reyes Restaurante at Wp.1

The walk starts in front of the **Reyes Restaurante** (Wp.1 0M), on the easternmost access road to **Roque del Faro**, signposted 'PR9 Los Andenes / Roque de los Muchachos'. We follow the side road (S) for 150 metres till it swings right and we maintain direction on a concrete track climbing past an apple orchard.

When the concrete gives way to dirt at a Y-junction, we bear left on a partially cobbled track passing a large goat pen. At the southern end of the goat pen (Wp.2 10M), we branch left on a dirt path descending into an affluent of the **Barranco de los Hombres**.

Crossing the bracken filled bed of the affluent, we ignore a clearer path to the left,

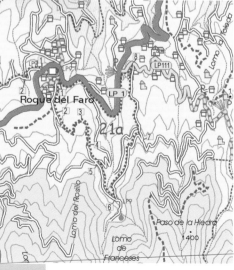

and turn right on an overgrown, grassy path climbing steeply between mesh fences choked with creepers. Bearing left when the path joins a minor dirt track, we climb gently (ENE) onto the **Lomo de Rosillo**, the spur separating the affluent from the main ravine. When the track crosses the nose of the spur and starts to descend (Wp.3 20M), we turn right on a broad trail carpeted with pine needles. Climbing gently (S) between huge pine, we pass a path branching left, then join a broad dirt track (Wp.4 25M).

Bearing left, we follow this dirt track into the **Barranco de los Hombres**, ignoring branches to left and right. At a Y-junction (Wp.5 30M), we stay on the main, level branch (right), a delightful forestry track lined with *laurisilva* and towering pine set against a backdrop of the distant rocks on the rim of the **Caldera**. A gentle stroll through peaceful woods, serenaded by blackbirds, brings us to a signposted junction, where we bear left, descending on a stretch of concrete to cross the *barranco* (Wp.6 40M).

The **PR9** turns right immediately after the bridge over the *barranco*, but we stay on the main track, winding round the contour lines (NE) surrounded by superb pine and with good views out to sea. Joining another track at a bend (Wp.7 50M), we bear left. Ignoring all branches, we follow this track down the **Lomo La Rama** (NNW), gradually coming into sight of **Roque del Faro**. We eventually join the old **Barlovento/Mimbreras** road (Wp.8 65M) which also doubles as part of the **PR9.1**. Bearing left, then left again 100 metres later, we return to our starting point via the main road, which is not nearly so long or steep as it looks from above, and carries very little traffic.

(b) Montaña de las Varas

A pleasant bucolic stroll and possible link to Walk 19. In theory, we follow the **SL50**, though at the time of writing, a large stretch of this is overgrown, obliging us to walk on tarmac for over a kilometre rather than a few hundred metres. To reach the start, turn north off the **Barlovento-Santo Domingo** road toward the **Ermita de San Antonio**, setting the odometer at 0. Turn right immediately, as if for **Juan Adalid**, then left at the Y-junction after 500 metres. The walk starts at km 1.1, at a crossroads with a dirt track, signposted 'SL50 Montaña de las Varas/Caldera de Agua'.

** Add 2 kilometres return if arriving by bus.
* There's a bar, not always open, just after the turning off the main road.

Access: by car & bus N° L11

The **SL50** dirt track (Wp.1 0M) heads east, soon dwindling to a grassy path passing between partially walled pasture and scrub. Ignoring a branch to the left, we cross a U-bend in another dirt track. Bearing right after the U (Wp.2 5M), we follow the track for fifty metres till it swings right and we take a branch track to the left.

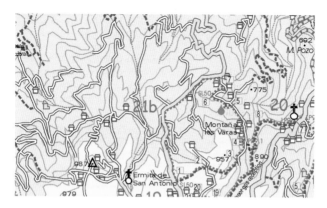

Ignoring a branch to the left fifty metres later, we start descending gently on a narrow path tunnelling through the trees. This lovely fairy-tale path winds down past small potato fields to a join a dirt track (Wp.3 15M), where we bear left and descend toward the sea. Ignoring a branch on the right to the 'PR9.1 Caldera de Agua/Don Pedro' (Wp.4 20M), we follow the signs for 'Montaña de las Varas', bearing left (NW) below a small farmstead, after which the track narrows and steepens. When the track enters another tree-tunnel section, look out for shallow earth steps to the left (Wp.5 30M). This slip path descends past a small well to rejoin the track twenty metres later.

Bearing left, we follow the track through banks of fern, crossing the **Barranco del Valle**, after which the track swings sharp right and an 'SL50' signpost (Wp.6 35M) beside a large prickly pear indicates a path branching left. Unfortunately, though signposted, this section was impassable when researched, so unless it has obviously been cleared, we stay on the dirt track until we rejoin the **Juan Adalid** lane (Wp.7 45M). From here a steady twenty minute climb up the lane, passing the official exit of the **SL50**, leads back to our starting point.

This was a classic walk long before the **GR130** was dreamed up and is now one of that path's most popular sections, rollercoasting along like a bucolic theme-ride through the hamlets, farms, and *barrancos* between **Barlovento** and **Gallegos**. There are several livestock gates en route: unless obviously propped open of tied back, shut them all.

| 4 | 2½ H | 6 km | | 400m / 300m | one way | 2* |

Extension: see Walk 23.

* in **Gallegos**

Access: by car and bus N° L11. To reach the start from the bus stop, take the main road up through **Barlovento**, following signs for the 'La Palma Romantica Hotel'.

Setting off along the tail of the T-junction at the south-western tip of **Barlovento** (Wp.1 0M), we follow the **Garafía** road, passing a turn-off for **Mirador de la Montaña del Molino**. Immediately after a large yellow house built above a tractor garage, we bear right on a concrete track (Wp.2 10M), superb views opening out along the undulating coast. When the concrete gives way to dirt (Wp.3 13M), we bear left on a broad dirt trail crossing a minor *barranco* to the *drago*-dotted hamlet of **La Tosca** (Wp.4 20M), where we join another concrete track. Bearing left at a Y-junction a couple of minutes later, we wind round the mountain to join another concrete track at a U-bend, where we bear right.

After a few minutes, the track swings sharp right (Wp.5 30M) and we maintain direction (W) on a concrete trail that soon dwindles to a partially paved path descending into the **Barranco de Topaciegas**. Passing immaculately maintained vines and vegetable patches, we reach our first gate and climb steadily onto a spur below a small house with a dragon tree (Wp.6 40M).

Joining another concrete track after a few minutes, we bear left and, fifty metres later, right on a dirt path (Wp.7 45M) in sight of **Roque de los Muchachos** observatory. A long, steady descent, takes us across **Barranco de la Vica** (Wp.8 55M) for, no great surprise, a comparably long, steady climb. After a second gate (Wp.9 60M), we reach a broad, very slightly vertiginous path, climbing into the hamlet of **La Palmita**, where we join a concrete track next to two large palm trees (Wp.10 65M).

Maintaining direction (W), we cross the main access track to the hamlet (the **SL40**, see Walk 24) (Wp.11 67M) and take a rough, narrow path below a farmhouse, zigzagging down into another mini-*barranco* before climbing steeply to join a dirt track (Wp.12 75M). Turning right, we cross another concrete track and, ignoring two branch tracks to the left, descend to a signposted path bearing left into the **Barranco de los Gallegos** (Wp.13 80M).

Going through another gate, we follow a broad dusty goat trail, descending past another very slightly vertiginous stretch, before zigzagging down steeply to the dry bed of the *barranco* (Wp.14 100M).

The path out of the *barranco* has been demolished by goats, but the way is reasonably clear, climbing steeply to another gate (Wp.15 110M) before crossing the concrete track (Wp.16 120M) leading to the hamlet of **La Crucita**, largely and loudly inhabited by barking dogs, within sight of **Gallegos**.

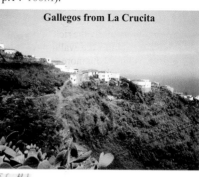

Gallegos from La Crucita

Zigzagging down past wild tomato plants, we cross the final *barranco*, passing a row of troglodytic cabins before climbing into the village opposite the **Bar Viveres** (Wp.17 130M), which certainly qualifies as *tipico*, though I'm not entirely sure what it's typical of! Still, it's worth stopping for a drink, especially on a Saturday afternoon, when burly farmers gather to watch Canal +, play the fruit machine, and cower in front of the barmaid. If there's time, it's worth exploring the village before following the access lane up to the main road for the bus (2pm to **Barlovento** & **Santa Cruz** / 4pm to **Santo Domingo**).

Despite a disproportionate amount of walking on concrete and tarmac, this little known circuit is a delightful introduction to the countryside around **Barlovento**, particularly the rich variety of trees that the region enjoys. Apart from one steep climb the walking is easy, making this an ideal route for relaxing after some of our more energetic itineraries.

* in **Barlovento**

Access: by car and bus N° L11

We start by following Walk 22 to Wp.11 (67M), where we turn left on the concrete track up to the main road (Wp.12 80M) passing a magnificent dragon tree en route. Bearing left, we follow the road for 500 metres into the **Barranco de la Vica**, where we turn right on a dirt track signposted 'SL40 Laguna de Barlovento' (Wp.13 90M).

The track climbs gently then steadily between the steepening walls of the *barranco*, flanked by shady heath, chestnut and laurel trees, sheltering throngs of songbirds. Passing a small cliff, we reach what appears to be a rubble tip, but is in fact an outlet for a *galería* (a tunnelled water canal). Going to the right of the larger works cabin (Wp.14 100M), we cross the *barranco* and climb narrow steps beside the smaller cabin.

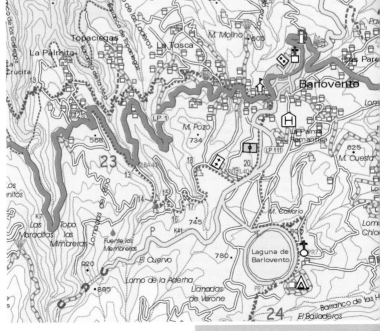

A shady path with occasional earth steps climbs steeply behind the cabin to the end of a grassy track (Wp.15 105M) leading to an orange grove. At the top of the grassy track we bear right on a concrete track, then left when this in turn joins a major dirt track (Wp.16 115M) in sight of **Montaña del Pozo** (on our left). Enjoying fine views of green hills backed by blue sea, we stroll past bushy laurel, heather, fern, the odd wild gladioli, pear trees and a cascade of blackberries.

Bearing right (Wp.17 125M) then left at successive Y-junctions, we follow the intermittently metalled track as it snakes round the head of **Barranco de Topaciegas** before climbing gently to a large green building (Wp.18 140M). Continuing on the main track, we ignore all branches and take the cemetery lane up to the *laguna*/**Fuente las Mimbreras** road (Wp.19 147M). Turning left, we follow the road for 150 metres and then turn left again (Wp.20 150M) on a broad back road passing the football ground. We then cross the **Mimbreras** road twice, the first time onto a dirt track that soon dwindles to a path, the second time onto a grassy track that rejoins the road seventy-five metres from our starting point.

On the whole, people responsible for PRs & GRs tend to stick to time-honoured trails, following old transhumance routes, royal ways and logging tracks, but here the pathmakers have done us proud, trailblazing a superb little path through the woods above **Barranco de la Herradura**, to give us a linear route through a typically and uniquely La Palman combination of tropical forest, misty heathland and tiny fields squeezed into the encroaching forest. There are fine views en route, though in all probability, these will be shrouded in cloud. Fortunately, the path is quite pretty enough of itself, whether you see anything beyond it or not.

| 4 | 3H 40M | 11.5 km | | 400m / 650m | one way | 4* |

Stroll: Wps. 1-6

* in **Los Sauces**

Short Version: (access by car) Wps. 6-12

Access: by bus N° L11. To reach the start, take the main road through **Barlovento**, following signs for 'La Palma Romantica'. Wp.1 is 75 metres after the LP1/LP111 T-junction.

We start 75 metres above the **Garafía** turn-off, on a grassy track (Wp.1 0M) between **Conjunto Residencial Tajinaste** and signs for the football field and cemetery. Climbing steadily, we cross the **Mimbreras** road (LP111) twice, the first time onto a path that broadens to a dirt track, the second onto a backroad climbing past the football ground. Rejoining the LP111 at a 'PR8/SL40' signpost (Wp.2 20M) we turn left then, fifty metres later, right on a concrete track. The track curves through a U-bend and we branch right on the second of two dirt tracks, which we follow till it joins the *laguna* road (Wp.3 30M). Leaving the **PR8**, we turn left and follow the road up to the *laguna*, an unprepossessing expanse of water collected in a fenced-off volcano crater.

If doing the full walk, you may wish to stay on the road round the *laguna* rather than take the following short but strenuous detour, in which case cut fifteen minutes from the overall time. Otherwise, turn left at the *laguna* on stone steps up to a small *mirador*. From the *mirador*, a dirt track runs parallel to the road, climbing steadily then steeply to the 800 metre trig point on

The *Parque Recreativo* at the *laguna*

Montaña del Calvario (Wp.4 40M), where we continue on a narrow path burrowing through vegetation to join a clearer path. Bearing left, we follow this path down to a dirt track, where we turn right and descend back to the *laguna*, just north of the open-air chapel/*plaza* (Wp.5 50M) used to celebrate local festivals.

Ignoring the 'Los Sauces PR7.1', we stay on the *laguna* road, passing the campsite, where there's a bar/restaurant. At the end of the metalled road, we bear right on a broad dirt path, the **Los Tilos PR7.1** (Wp.6 55M), climbing roughly-hewn steps. Ignoring a branch track to the right, we join a broad dirt track, fifty metres along which we turn left (Wp.7 60M), still following the 'Los Tilos' signposts. The track dips into **Barranco de las Hijas**, where we turn left (Wp.8 75M) on a stepped path under an immense walnut tree. After a steep climb we join a narrow dirt track beside an apple orchard. Turning right and then left 75 metres later, we pass between the apple orchard and a plum orchard, before bearing right at a Y-junction (Wp.9 85M). A steady climb past a melon patch leads to a small clearing and a signposted path descending SW (Wp.10 90M).

The path, fenced with rough railings, descends the steep, densely forested **Ladera de Guerreros** into the first complex folds of the **Barranco de la Herradura**, crossing a footbridge below an ochre-stained spring mottled with lichen (Wp.11 95M). Climbing away from the spring, we pass the first of two wickerwork cabin frames, before descending again, negotiating a few metres where the railings have collapsed and the path is crumbling away. Following the folds of the *barranco*, we cross a *galería* pipe, passing a large works hut (Wp.12 110M) and a source tunnel.

Winding through the woods (SE), we join a rough dirt track, where we bear right, climbing below a large bluff undermined by a couple of caves. The track levels out amid huge ferns before climbing gently above the main *barranco*.

Passing in and out of shade, we wind round watersheds and affluent gullies, crossing a small mudslide where the track narrows to a path (Wp.13 135M), finally joining the **PR7** *pista forestal* from **Pico de la Cruz** (Wp.14 150M).

Turning left ,we follow this track virtually all the way to **Los Sauces**, ignoring all but two branches, the first being the turning for **Mirador de las Baranda** or **del Topo de la Baranda** (Wp.15 160M), a five minute excursion from the main track and well worth it, if the **Barranco del Agua** and **Los Tilos** aren't under cloud. Returning to the main track we continue our descent, again ignoring all branches until we pass a large camouflaged reservoir, shortly after which we bear right (Wp.16 190M) on a steep, well-paved shortcut, rejoining the track at another *mirador* a few minutes later. Maintaining direction (E), we pass a large antenna and descend steeply toward **Los Sauces**, first on concrete then on tarmac. In the built up area, we follow the main tarmac lane down to the town square.

The bus stop is to the left, next to the church, the taxi stand (roughly €10 to **Barlovento**) to the right on the western side of the square.

In one form or another, this is a 'must-do' for <u>every</u> visitor. Setting off from the **Casa del Monte** (1280 metres) we follow the **Los Tilos** canal round the head of the **Barranco Rivero** (later **del Agua**) to the **Marcos** and **Cordero** sources, traversing 13 tunnels en route. We then descend the ravine through the jungle-like **Tilos** forest to the **Visitors' Centre** access road. And for once, 'descent' does not imply diminishing returns. Every step of the way, we are surprised by constantly unfolding and improving views, while the *laurisilva* forest gets deeper, denser and greener to the very end. Not for a moment does it disappoint, and I strongly recommend the full walk, though the short versions both qualify as 'must-dos', too.

The only drawback is that the full walk involves taking a 4x4 taxi (see **Access** details below) and having a car at the end. The dirt track from **Las Lomadas** to **Casa del Monte** (signposted 'Nacimientos de Marcos y Cordero' in the village, thereafter 'Casa del Monte') is passable without 4x4 and plenty of lightweight, short-wheelbase cars make it – though more than a few <u>don't</u> and the rental company may be a bit miffed if you limp into the airport with a treadless, bottomless, clutchless paddle-car. The track is rough and dusty and, though re-stabilised each year (generally in time for the elections!), subject to erosion. You could combine this with the classic waterfall stroll up the **Barranco de Agua** (join one of the guided parties - €2 a head - when the dry waterfall is reanimated).

Equipment: many people wear trainers, but boots are best; <u>A TORCH IS ESSENTIAL</u> as some of the tunnels are very long and very dark; <u>A WATERPROOF CAPE IS STRONGLY RECOMMENDED</u> as it's raining in tunnel number twelve – all the time, very heavily. Although we follow a canal perched high above the ravine, the risk of vertigo is minimal, as the path is wide and the most vertiginous stages are fenced with railings. In fact, there's a bigger risk of claustrophobia than vertigo. That said, do not (this isn't a joke, you'd be surprised how many people do this) lean over railings to 'get a good photo' of yourself. There's a risk of rockslides after or during heavy rains. The only other danger is the obvious one of clouting your head on low tunnel roofs. The way is well waymarked and obvious. The water in the canal is for drinking, so no dipping in to refresh yourself on a hot day. The short walk to **Mirador de Espigón Atravesado** is easy though the *mirador* itself is <u>very</u> vertiginous.

Please note that due to poor reception, no waypoints are given for this route.

** but allow 4-5 hours   * at the Los Tilos Visitors' Centre

Short Versions
(a) To Wp.3, returning the same way
(b) In reverse to the **Mirador de Espigón Atravesado**

Access: 4x4 taxi and car. I recommend taking **Pepe's 4x4 taxi**, **Tel: 649 945481** (or enquire at the **Cafeteria Sisigam Tel: 922 451775 in Los Sauces**).

Pepe doesn't speak English, but the **Tourist Information Office** can help non-Spanish speakers. The minimum trip-fare is €50, but the price drops if you share; a full taxi (6 people) comes out at €25 per couple. During the summer, the height of the domestic tourism season, there's a good chance you'll find yourself in a full taxi. In winter, you may have to wait for the weekend. Arrange to meet at the end of the **PR6**, km 2.4 of the **Los Tilos** access road, where there's a lay-by, mapboard, and small car-park. It's worthwhile popping into the **Visitors' Centre** the day before.

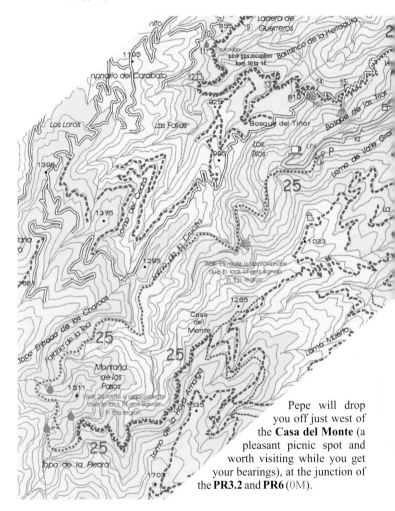

Pepe will drop you off just west of the **Casa del Monte** (a pleasant picnic spot and worth visiting while you get your bearings), at the junction of the **PR3.2** and **PR6** (0M).

We take the broad canal path (SW), signposted 'Entrada por El Canal a Marcos y Cordero 4.5km 13 túneles'. Winding alongside the canal with *laurisilva* 'blinkers' to our right, we glimpse **Barranco Rivero** through the trees before rounding a bend to a stretch of railings and our first superb views across the ravine. Italic numbers after walking times are the minutes required to traverse longer tunnels. Short tunnels are given no traverse time.

Tunnel No.1 (8M *3M*) is easy at first as we walk on top of the canal, but gets lower halfway along, obliging us to drop down alongside the canal. After the much shorter and easier **Tunnel No. 2** (17M), we reach a slightly vertiginous section with railings. We then duck under a large toppled pine, after which views open out behind us down the *barranco* to its confluence with the **Cordero** watercourse. **Tunnel No.3** (24M *8M*), which has a small cave at its mouth, is the longest and most intimidating – you certainly wouldn't want to bump into anything hairy down there! After 30 metres, puddles appear underfoot and the roof dips down. The tunnel gets lower and tighter as the canal wall gets higher.

Finally, we glimpse daylight, but have to bend over sideways, possibly even taking off a bulky rucksack, as the roof slopes further in. We finally emerge on a small ledge and immediately duck into the short but very low **Tunnel No. 4**. Crossing a bridge over a small ravine, we come to **Tunnel No.5** (38M). At first the way is reasonably well lit by windows, but soon darkens and narrows, forcing us to squeeze between the tunnel wall and canal, before emerging briefly then ducking into **Tunnel No.6** (43M), which, like its predecessor, is about 75 metres long. **Tunnels No.7 & 8** (45M & 48M), are short and require no torch.

Tunnel No. 9 (49M) is longer, but reasonably lit. It narrows halfway along, forcing us to bend double and walk on the canal wall. Back in the open, we descend round a holding tank before continuing on a narrow, railed path. **Tunnel No. 10** (57M) is short, but curves so we need the torch. **Tunnel No. 11** (59M) is well lit by windows and soon emerges on a narrow railed balcony, where we hear the roar of water and see the waterfall lined path climbing above the **Nacimiento de Marcos**.

Tunnel No.12 (61M *3M*) is where we don our waterproofs. This may seem prissy, but it's raining in there, heavily, so it's either waterproofs or duck and run. You may find plastic bin bags here, though that depends on which way the last group went. Climbing over a small sluice gate onto a narrow overflow path, we go through the rain, pausing if it's not too cold to enjoy the view through windows curtained by sheets of water.

We now pass the **Marcos** source and climb steeply on deep stone steps alongside the roaring waters descending from the **Cordero**. After a second, slightly less steep climb on stone steps, we join the **Cordero** canal (71M). Strolling along the canal, we come to our last tunnel, **No.13** (74M), which looks easy but is studded with head clouting protuberances. We soon hear roaring water again as we approach the **Nacimiento de Cordero** (80M) where we begin our descent.

Bearing right, a steep, stepped descent brings us down to the dry **Cordero** watercourse, where we duck under a fallen tree and cross a rockspill to pass the signposted junction with the **SL30**, a path which even the Spanish say is 'very dangerous' (85M). Our path drops down, switching onto the right bank of the watercourse, which falls away to our left. Gradually descending through pine to the denser *laurisilva*, we recross the watercourse (90M). After passing a second dangerous-path, another of the many stepped descents brings us back into the bed of the *barranco* (95M), which we follow for the next fifteen minutes.

Hopping from boulder to boulder and levering ourselves down waterchutes, we descend between cliffs cloaked with moss, ivy, houseleeks and shrubby *laurisilva*. After ten minutes, we come to a narrower section where a trodden dirt path winds through the boulders and debris of fallen trees passing marvellous giant ferns (105M).

The *barranco* broadens slightly and we come to a waypost, where we bear right before crossing a footbridge (110M) back onto the *barranco's* left bank, which we follow on a good dirt path for most of the descent down the wooded slopes of the **Fajana de la Tea**.

Alternating level stretches and descents, during which the watercourse drops away steeply below us and views open out across the *barranco*, lead to a broad fenced ledge forming a natural *mirador* (115M), after which we pass a slightly vertiginous section before crossing the first of several affluent watersheds. The forest gradually closes in and we begin our final, steep descent, passing a small, stagnant *fuente* (135M). The descents continue, and the further down we go, the deeper the forest becomes. The path finally swings right to cross a footbridge over the **Barranco del Agua** (150M), beyond which a brief climb brings us onto a broad dirt trail, where we bear left.

This trail is a delight, winding down the valley on a beautifully mottled carpet of dead leaves, tunnelling through towering trees festooned with hanging creepers, and passing ferns so huge they dwarf even the giants seen higher up the ravine. We soon come to the **Mirador de Espigón Atravesado** location board (160M). You'll understand why the board's not actually on the *mirador* if you take the stepped branch on the right just after the board, a five minute diversion (counted in subsequent timings) that I strongly recommend. The branch path weaves between railings and thin walls of rock along an incredibly narrow ridge till it reaches the *mirador*, a tiny fenced ledge (room for about 4 people who really like each other) suspended above nothing.

N.B. If you're doing the short version to the *mirador*, it's worth continuing on the broad trail a little further after Wp.11 to see more of the forest. After visiting the *mirador*, we simply follow the main trail back to the **Los Tilos** access road, passing a small cabin swallowed by vegetation (175M) and an information board (185M) about the **Til** or Greenheart tree that gives the reserve its name. After going through a 'train' tunnel, we bear left and descend to the parking area (195M).

The **Barranco de la Galga** forest, popularly known as the 'Cubo' or bucket, is like **Los Tilos** writ small. It's not as impressive as its big neighbour - very little is - but it's sufficiently remarkable to be one of the island's minor classics and would, anywhere less blessed with *barrancos*, be trumpeted to the skies as a stunningly unique phenomenon, dressed up with Visitors' Centres, restaurants, picnic areas, car-parks and coach loads of camcorders. On La Palma, it's hidden away up a scruffy unmarked dirt track tucked between a couple of tunnels. So much the better! For some reason I can't quite fathom, this is usually treated as two-way linear walk, which is a pity, since the **PR5.1** is a near perfect loop, marred only by a kilometre on the main road, and even that can be avoided by judicious use of the buses or going as a two-car party (see Access). The path is not always well waymarked and there's one area where storm damage calls for some energetic scrambling over felled trees, but the route is straightforward and, bar the road, always engaging.

Please note that due to poor GPS reception, no waypoints are given for this route.

3/4* | 2H 10M ** | 7 km | 400m / 400m | ○ | 3

* 4 in its present state, 3 if the fallen trees
  are cleared.
** but (allow 3 hours)

Access: by car and bus N° L11. If two cars are available leave one at **Casa Asterio Restaurant** and start the Walk at the 10 minute point. If arriving by bus, ask to be dropped off at **Barranco de la Galga**, though the new tunnel makes this a little hazardous so drivers may refuse.

If you haven't been able to arrange direct access to **Barranco de la Galga**, the walk starts from **La Galga** bus-stop (0M) at the turn-off for the **Mirador** and **Ermita de San Bartolome**, 700 metres from **Barranco de la Galga**. Heading north along the main road, we stay on the left, facing the oncoming traffic, until we round a bend and see the first tunnel.

One hundred metres from the tunnel, we cross (very carefully and very quickly) onto the seaward side of the road. Following a partially paved track alongside the road, we approach the tunnel, where we take the old road round the outside of the tunnel. Having by-passed the tunnel, we cross the road (again C&Q!) and take the dirt track (10M) on the left (SW). When the main track swings left after thirty metres to pass under the road, we bear right on the branch track up the *barranco*.

The track climbs steadily, soon passing impressive cliffs (S), after which chestnut trees and *laurisilva* start to crowd in on either side. We wind up the *barranco*, our steady climb interrupted by a succession of brief level stretches, from one of which we can see a second high cliff to the south, this one pierced by *galería* 'windows' along the **Canal del Estado**. After passing under an aqueduct (30M), we continue our steady climb, crossing and re-

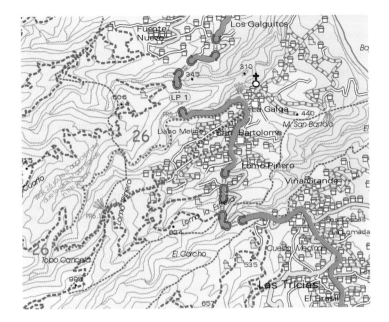

crossing the watercourse seven times before the main track veers north and we turn sharp left (45M), traversing roughly levelled land to take a rough path up the *barranco*.

The path climbs up the right bank of the watercourse then bears left, crossing a small clearing and winding through thick ferns to pass under a small aqueduct, fifty metres after which we come to a T-junction with another path. Turning right, we climb steadily on log-retainer steps, passing an improvised *área recreativa* (the blue bunting visible fifty metres to your right), after which the path runs into a muddied section lined with railings (55M). At the end of a second stretch of railings (separated from the first by a gap of a few metres), we have to negotiate the first fallen trees.

More steady climbing brings us to a third set of railings, at the end of which a tiny dirt path (60M) doubles back to the right, descending into a miniature gorge in the bed of the *barranco*. The path is steep and slippery, but I recommend a five minute diversion down to the cleft: canopied by tall trees, fringed with fern, dripping with water, stained with rust, and bearded with lichen and moss, some so heavily leafed it resembles seaweed, it is a spectacular little place.

Continuing on the main path, we cross more dramatic storm damage, either to the right (the official route) or to the left where ramblers have trodden a way –neither route is easy! We rejoin the undamaged path along another railed section, after which we cross the watercourse (75M including diversion) onto the left bank. Winding through dense woodland, we switch back onto the right bank and climb to join a dirt track (80M) where we turn left for **Mirador de Somada Alta**.

A long gentle climb, passing two branches to the left and one to the right, brings us behind the **Mirador de Somada Alta** (95M), a curiously elaborate structure of step, tunnel and terrace. Bearing left and leaving the track, we can either go under the footbridge to join the descending path immediately, or cross the footbridge and descend to the location/information board at the *mirador's* tip to enjoy the view, from where we double back on the lower terrace to join the path down to **La Galga**.

The path zigzags down to join an old trail, running alongside a silver waterpipe in a deep trench-like cutting. Crossing a narrow dirt track (100M), we continue following the silver pipe, at first on a narrow dirt track, then in the trench-trail again. After a steep descent, we emerge below a small house on a concrete driveway, which we descend to cross a concrete track (105M) and a branch dirt track, below which we bear left, back into our trench-trail. The trail then broadens into a concrete track (**Calle Fuente Pino**, only signposted below) which, unless taking the alternative descent, we follow all the way down to **La Galga** and the main road. The concrete track crosses a tarmac lane twice (110M & 115M).

For the alternative version descending directly to the bus-stop
Turn left after crossing the tarmac lane the second time at 115 minutes, then right one hundred metres later on a signposted path, leading to a waymarked route that eventually emerges at the bus stop.

For refreshment, stay on the concrete track after 115 minutes till it emerges on the main road opposite the **Casa Asterio Restaurant** (125M) - a bit of a barn, vast and graceless, but the food's good. The restaurant is 400 metres south of the bus stop.

Once you've driven up to the **Roque de los Muchachos** (The Lads' Rock, and the highest point on the island) and done your obligatory gasping, you may question the attractions of trudging along the barren rim of the **Caldera**. But pottering about in a car-park can never match walking to give a sense of place and every new approach to the rim is an eye-opener. This short itinerary, which never strays far from the road, is one of those rare walks that are easy yet take you through decidedly uneasy terrain.

If walking in winter, wrap up warm. In summer, sunscreen and a hat are essential. Not recommended in wet or windy weather. Very slight risk of vertigo.

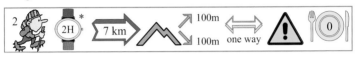

2 | 2H | 7 km | 100m / 100m one way | ⚠ | 0

.* +1 hour for gawping!)

Access: by car/TF$. There are several roadside parking spaces to the east of Wp.1.

> **Strolls**
>
> To **Pico de la Cruz** from Wp.1, **Pared de Roberto** from Wp.5

We start at km 28.5 of the **Santa Cruz - Hoya Grande** road, on a paved stairway for 'Pico de la Cruz PR7/8' (Wp.1 0M), which almost immediately joins the **GR131 Ruta de la Crestería** (Wp.2). The main walk is to the right, but it's worth turning left first, either to visit the natural *mirador* at the end of the trodden path ten metres from the junction, or to follow the GR up to **Pico de la Cruz** (Wp.3 10M) for superb views over the **Caldera** and across the sea of clouds to Tenerife, La Gomera and El Hierro.

... across waymarked rocks

Returning to the **GR131/PR7** junction, we pick our way (W) across waymarked rocks onto a clear path climbing behind a small rise. Descending toward the road, we pass a signpost for the 'Barranco del Diablo' and 'Barranco del Gallegos' (Wp.4 30M), then climb a shallow broom-covered slope before re-descending to the road at the **Degollada de Franceses Mirador** (Wp.5 45M) where we continue on a narrow dirt path. From a distance, this path appears to cross a sheer red slope before petering out. In fact, it's not nearly so alarming as it looks from afar.

The point at which it appears to peter out is the gateway through the **Pared de Roberto** (Wp.6 47M), one of the natural basaltic walls that are such a distinctive feature of the **Caldera**.

Legend has it that a young man used to cross the *cumbre* to visit his girlfriend. Jealous of their love, the devil, who seems to have spent a lot of time gadding about these parts, manifested himself as Roberto and threw up this 'insurmountable' wall, blocking the young man's path. 'Roberto' then proposed a Faustian pact, making a gateway in exchange for his victim's soul. To be honest, our hapless lover was either no great climber or prized his soul over-lightly, but the deal was done and the gateway remains.

After the gateway, we continue along the GR, climbing before dropping down to another natural *mirador* (Wp.7 60M). We then cross another small rise before winding past then branching right to the **Mirador de Andenes** (Wp.8 70M). Unless possessed of a compelling urge to climb to a car-park, we return the same way.

This is the rugged end of the crater and, in pure walking terms, perhaps the most interesting stretch of path on the rim, winding between rocks, dipping up and down, changing all the time, and eventually climbing to a unique outlook on the island's question mark spine.

| 3 | 1H 40M | 6 km | | 300m 300m | two way | 0 |

Access: by car/TF$. The walk starts at km 2.9 of the Observatory access road, a little over 500 metres west of **Roque de los Muchachos**, on a dirt track branching south. There's parking for three cars next to the mapboard of the descent to **Torre del Time**.

Short Version: to Wp.5

Stroll: to Wp.2

The dirt track, the Observatory visible

From the road (Wp.1 0M), we follow the dirt track for a few metres before bearing right on the broad, GR-waymarked path we will follow to the base of **Roque Palmero**. The path runs parallel to the dirt track before passing two drum-like satellite dishes and bearing west to a small weather-hut. We then pass a sign for the 'Barrancos de Hoyo Verde' and 'Izcagua', and skirt round the base of **Roque Chico** (Wp.2 10M).

We now descend to a signpost for the 'Barranco de Marangaño' (Wp.3 15M), just before which it's worth bearing left a few metres to a natural *mirador* over-looking the crater towards La Gomera. Returning to the GR, a short, steady climb crosses a craggy, unnamed peak, after which we skirt behind a larger bluff, the **Morro de la Crespa** (Wp.4 20M).

Crossing a small rise backed by a broad firebreak, we pass a stubby, battered geodesic survey post (Wp.5 30M), from where we have superb views into the **Barranco de Bombas de Agua**, flanked by small basaltic walls you'd swear were man-made, and enough shades of brown to shame a Flemish Old Master.

A rough, rocky descent brings us down to the **Degollada de las Palomas** (Wp.6 35M) dividing the **Barrancos de Bombas de Agua** and **de Garome**. Continuing in a southerly direction, we cross two outcrops of rock, the first relatively large and topped by boulders, the second no more than a thin angled shelf poking through the path.

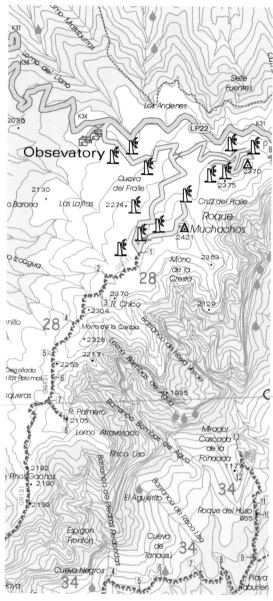

Immediately after the second outcrop, we leave the GR, turning left on a faint trodden way marked by two large cairns and a GR cross (Wp.7 40M). The cairn-marked way climbs steadily, weaving through the scrub to the trig point on the very rocky **Roque Palmero** (Wp.8 50M), from where we have good views over the **Caldera** and **Cumbres Nueva** and **Vieja**.

We return via the same route, resisting the temptation to take a slip path round the nameless peak south of Wp.3 (narrow path, steep slope, abrupt drop = flat head!).

This stretch of the **Caldera**'s rim is perhaps the most photogenic and many postcards, notably early morning shots of the crater full of cloud, are taken from the photo-spots mentioned in the text. Following the **GR131**, we wind round the small peaks of the north-eastern rim, peering into deep *barrancos* defined by narrow pinnacles of rock, and gazing at the varicoloured strata underpinning the lip of the crater.

3 | 2H 40M | 9 km | 200m / 200m | two way | 0

Short Versions	**Extension**
To the 'photo-spots' at Wps. 4&5	If you come by taxi, arrange to meet at **Pista Pico de la Nieve**, combining this itinerary with Walk 30 – allow 2½-3 hours including stops.
Stroll: to **Pico de la Cruz**	

Access: see Walk 27

We start as in Walk 27, at km 28.5 of the **Santa Cruz - Hoya Grande** road, on the paved stairway for 'Pico de la Cruz PR7/8', from the **PRs 7&8** mapboard (Wp.1 0M). We climb onto the **GR131** and bear left for a short, steady ascent to **Pico de la Cruz** (Wp.2 10M). From the peak, we descend (E) across a rock-filled hollow onto a clear dirt path winding along the crest towards the distant 'agave' sculpture.

The PR Mapboard start

Skirting a small rise, we briefly lose sight of the crater, before climbing onto a second small rise topped with a rocky outcrop (Wp.3 25M), immediately after which, we pass the first photo-spot (Wp.4).

Winding along a section where the narrow rim is sandwiched between the road and the crater, we pass the second photo-spot (Wp.5 35M). Neither are physically distinct, but the views are all the identification they require.

We then climb gently, passing a signpost (Wp.6 42M) for 'Barranco de los Guanches' (in the crater) and 'Barranco de la Fuente Vizcaino' (E). After passing a little way below the peak's trig point, we reach a sign for 'Pico de Piedrallana' (Wp.7 45M), from where we have stunning views over the

Barranco de Altaguna. Our path now zigzags down over light volcanic rock to the first of two watersheds feeding the *barranco*. We then skirt the small top separating us from the second, signposted watershed, where there's also a sign for 'Barranco Hondo' (E) (Wp.8 65M). Climbing between large boulders, we pass a distinctive oblong block of rock, shortly after which a trodden way bears right to a natural *mirador* (Wp.9 70M).

The cloud-filled crater

Continuing on the main path, we skirt behind the small **Pico del Cedro**, before a short, easy climb brings us onto the bare **Pico de la Nieve** (Wp.10 80M). We return via the same route.

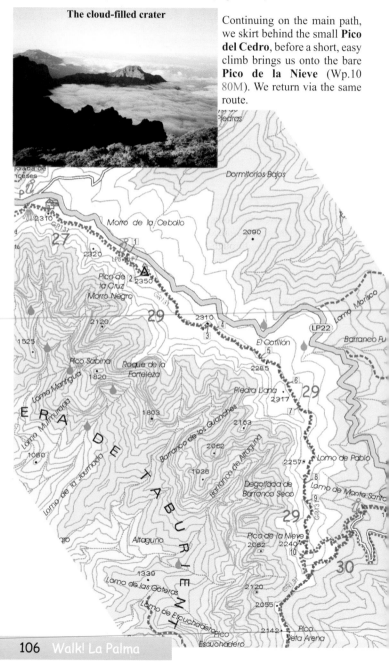

30 PICO DE LA NIEVE

This easy route on clear paths is one of the few practical ascents of the **Caldera** to give a sense of actually climbing somewhere, most of the other ways to the top either being too short to count or too long for comfort. The outlook across the crater is all the better for being reached on foot. The usual recommendations apply: cover up as befits the season and beware of the wind – the summit is very exposed.

Access: by car/TF\$. We start from the **Santa Cruz-Roque de los Muchachos** road, at the junction with the *pista forestal* to 'Pico de la Nieve 1.9km'. Park on the southern side of the track for shade.

Short Version

Drive to the end of the dirt track (Wp.2)

Taking the **PR3** (Wp.1 0M) just north of the *pista forestal*, we climb long, shallow steps alongside the road before switching back on a gentler slope through the pine woods.

Climbing the long, shallow steps

The path becomes a broad trail marked with regular cairns, climbing steadily to the turning circle at the end of the *pista forestal* (Wp.2 20M).

Staying behind the turning circle, we take the path above the *pista*, passing a mapboard and crossing a dry watercourse. Climbing steadily again, we pass a small wooden cross with a corroded commemorative plaque (Wp.3 25M), then turn right at a signposted junction (Wp.4 30M) for 'Pico de la Nieve/Roque de los Muchachos'. Climbing through the last scattered pine to the broom covered slopes below the peak, we come into sight of **Santa Cruz**, the **Cumbre Vieja**, Tenerife and La Gomera, then El Hierro, and finally the southern part of the crater and **Pico Bejenado**. Joining the **GR131** (Wp.5 50M) on the crest, we turn right to reach the bleak, windswept peak (Wp.6 55M).

Retracing our steps to the **GR131/PR3** junction, we head south along the crest, passing a small natural windbreak. The GR descends on a rocky path partially overgrown with broom, passing behind a small rise onto a more densely overgrown but still discernible stretch leading to the junction with our return route (Wp.7 70M), signposted 'Pista Pico de la Nieve/Salida'. This narrow path descends gently then follows the contours of the mountain with fine views over **Santa Cruz**, rejoining our outward route at Wp.4 (80M).

We can now either follow the same route back to the start, or take a rough slip path (Wp.8 85M) just before the dry watercourse 150 metres from Wp.2, and descend along the dirt track.

The **Cumbrecita** is at the end of the only asphalted road into the **Caldera** (other than the narrow lane into the **Barranco de las Angustias** - see Walk 33) and is popular with sightseers, so get there early - by 10 o'clock so many cars are shunting back and forth it resembles the lower deck of a ferry. Don't be discouraged, though. This walk is an excellent introduction to the interior of the **Caldera**, taking us past a series of pictorial information boards explaining the crater's formation and ecology.

The loop round the *miradors* is within the range of all walkers. The canal path is not. It's narrow, <u>extremely vertiginous</u>, has no safety barriers, and is potentially very dangerous, being subject to rockslides and the 'dry' erosion of summer, when the soil is so friable it can no longer sustain its own weight and one dislodged pebble is enough to create a significant landslip. The path is regularly repaired, but not necessarily every year, so inquire about conditions beforehand. Do not venture onto this path when it is wet or windy.

Access: by car

Stroll	Short Version
To the **Mirador de las Chozas**	Without the canal (1 hour; see Wp.8)

From the higher of the two **Cumbrecita** car-parks (Wp.1 0M), we cross the lower car-park and take a broad dirt track (W), which we follow all the way to the **Lomo de las Chozas** *mirador*. Strolling along and pausing to inspect the ceramic information boards, we pass the **Mirador de los Roques** path doubling back on the right (Wp.2 15M). Continuing along the track to circle the 'island' at the end of the *lomo*, we descend to the *mirador* (Wp.3 20M), where we have excellent views of **Lomo de los Bueyes**, behind which is the park campsite.

The broad dirt track

Returning to Wp.2, we descend gently on a narrow path, the vegetation around us an object lesson in the flora panels seen on the track. After crossing two footbridges (Wps.4&5 35M & 40M), we climb two brief flights of steps to join the canal path (Wp.6 45M), where we bear left to **Mirador de los**

Roques (Wp.7 47M). The views from here are even better, and we can pick out the thin silver thread of the **Cascada de la Fondada** (NW) above the broad fin-like **Roque de Huso** (see Walk 34).

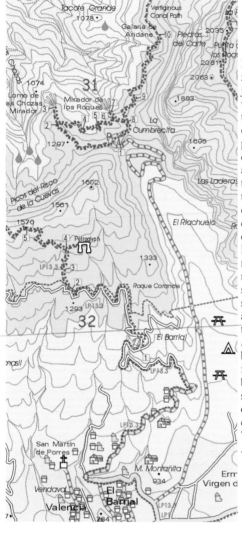

Returning to Wp.7, we zigzag up to a signposted junction (Wp.8 55M) where we turn right for the **Cumbrecita** (60M) or bear left for the canal path, signposted 'Zona de Acampada' (do not attempt to continue on the canal directly from the *mirador*). The path crosses a small rise then descends to rejoin the canal (Wp.9 60M). Following the canal as it ripples round the mountainside, we pass several vertiginous stretches with views that are even better than those from the official *miradors*. Curving into a broad, very precipitous fold, we are confronted by an undulating drop of striated rock, that must once have been an extraordinary waterfall. This is the **Galería de Aridane** (Wp.10 80M).

It's possible to continue along the canal, usually as far as **Hoyo de los Pinos** or **Lomo de Escuchadero** if not all the way to the campsite, but I suggest turning back here. The drops should have been quite enough for anyone by this stage.

Bejenado is the solitary peak at the southern end of the **Caldera**. Though not unusually high, its singular position makes it one of the best *miradors* in La Palma, no small distinction on an island boasting an embarrassment of outstanding views. The path, which is straightforward and well-waymarked (yellow-and-white stripes), is so gradually staged, one barely notices the climb. Walking shoes or trainers are adequate. Not to be done on hot, windy days when there's a risk of fire.

Short Version: to **El Rodeo**

Access: by car
Set the odometer at zero at the start of the LP-202 into the **Parque Nacional**. Ignore branches to **Virgen del Pino** and **Cumbrecita** (km0.8 & km1) and follow the main road, **Carrer de Valencia**, through the **El Barrial** *urbanización*. At km4.5 the tarmac ends. Ignoring **Calle Valencia** to the right, continue on the main dirt track, **Pista de Valencia**, signposted 'PR13.3 Bejenado'. At km5.8 the tarmac resumes. Park round the next corner (km6) at a mapboard detailing the route.

From the parking area (Wp.1 0M), we take the dirt track (**Pista Ferrer**) climbing to the left, soon coming into sight of **Bejenado**. Ignoring all branches, we follow the main track as it bears west, until we reach a signposted junction (Wp.2 25M), where we leave the track and climb to the right (N) on a pine-needle covered trail. The itinerary is driveable to Wp.2, but the walk starts lower down to avoid congestion on a track that could, literally, be vital in the event of fire. Even Spaniards, who generally don't get out of their car till it's tipping over a precipice, seem to respect the norm.

The trail soon dwindles to a path (Wp.3 30M) winding steadily up a broad spur defined by two gullies. At another signposted junction (Wp.4 35M) we bear right for a five minute diversion to visit the 'petroglyphs' … well, one actually and that's behind bars, but it's only 120 metres away so you may as well visit it! Returning to Wp.4, we cross the westernmost gully defining the spur and continue climbing steadily (NW), crossing and, in one case, re-crossing three more gullies, the third of which, below the **Risco de las Cuevas**, is distinguished by a quadruple watershed (Wp.5 65M).

The Caldera from El Rodeo

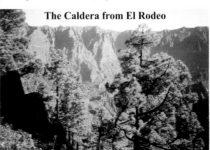

Ignoring a faint cairn-marked branch to the right, we climb to **El Rodeo** (Wp.6 80M), a natural balcony from where we have our first stunning views of the **Caldera**.

Continuing our steady climb on a narrower, rougher path, we zigzag up the back of the peak, bringing Tenerife, La Gomera and El Hierro into view. After climbing through more switchbacks than I'd care to count, we come to a longish, north-easterly stretch, crossing a final gully (Wp.7 105M).

The remaining long zigzags lead us up to the crest, which is mildly vertiginous, and the peak (Wp.8 120M), where we have a superb panorama over the **Caldera**, including the sacred pinnacle of **Roque Idafe**.

On the crest

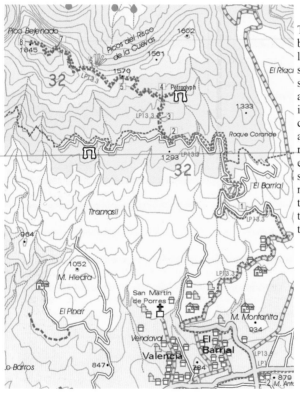

The branch path below **El Rodeo** leads into a small loop, but since the park authorities are increasingly concerned about locating ramblers in the event of fire and specifically request we stick to the marked trails, we return the same way.

33 BARRANCO DE LAS ANGUSTIAS - CASCADA DE COLORES

A classic route up the aptly named **Barranco de las Angustias**, literally 'Ravine of Anguishes', more pithily translated as 'Gorge of Fear': either way, you get the picture. This is the supreme ravine on an island of ravines, worn through the western wall of the **Caldera** before the crater's water was canalised. Canals notwithstanding, freak flash floods are not unknown, so check the forecast at the Visitors' Centre first. The *cascada* is a small waterfall stained by deposits from the ferruginous water. The described route follows the official path, which is well signposted, but staying in the bed of the *barranco* is an enjoyable alternative in summer (see text).

* including the return

Access: by car/4X4T

From **Los Llanos de Aridane**, follow the signs for 'Barranco de las Angustias'. Shortly after the park information cabin, set the odometer at zero. The road into the *barranco* now has a tarmac surface, but is steep, narrow and winding, requiring nerve and concentration. Park alongside the bed of the *barranco* after 2.2km. Ask at the tourist office for 4X4 taxis or see the Appendices at the back of this book.

Strolls & Short Versions
Given that it's a linear route, these are discretionary, but obvious turning points are Wps. 5, 7, & 11.

The walk starts 150 metres later on a narrow path along the left bank of the *barranco*, marked with a 'PR13' signpost and, more usefully since these signs continue inside the park, a green panel for 'zona de acampada' (Wp.1 0M). The path soon joins a dirt track, which we follow (NE) into the *barranco*. When the track passes under an aqueduct and climbs north, we stay in the *barranco* (Wp.2 10M).

Trudging up the gravelly bed of the increasingly narrow ravine, we criss-cross a meagre, weedy rivulet then, 100 metres after a tiny affluent trickling down a stepped cascade to our right, take a signposted path on the right bank (Wp.3 25M). Ignoring a rough track branching left a few metres later, we cross the affluent **Barranco del Fraile** (Wp.4 30M) then the main watercourse (Wp.5 35M). Climbing onto the left bank, we pass a tiny spring and an overgrown path up to a small house on the right (visible from lower down, but not from the junction).

Our path returns to the *barranco*, passing under an aqueduct, forty metres after which, we bear left (Wp.6 45M) and cross a canal leading to the aqueduct. After a steady climb, the path levels out, passing the **Morro de la Era** cabin and crossing a dry torrent streaked with stains. Re-crossing the *barranco* (Wp.7 60M), we climb very slightly through pine and prickly pear before a stretch of concrete descends to a rockface daubed, somewhat excessively, with 'campada/acampada' graffiti (Wp.8 65M). Fifty metres later we bear right, crossing the **Lomo de La Rosera** (Wp.9 70M).

The path rejoins the streambed (and it is a stream by now) just before a piped aqueduct fitted with slats to serve as a footbridge. We go under the aqueduct (Wp.10 85M) and follow the stream, the weed already rusty with iron deposits, passing a small white waterhut squeezed under a huge boulder. From here, we can either take the signposted path along the watercourse's raised right bank or stay beside the stream for 150 metres until we reach the turbine hut and dam at **Dos Aguas**, where we climb through the trees to the left of the dam. In either case, we emerge in a large open area just behind the dam where the **Río Taburiente** and **Barranco Almendro Amargo** ('bitter almonds') run into one another to form the **Barranco de la Angustias** (Wp.11 100M).

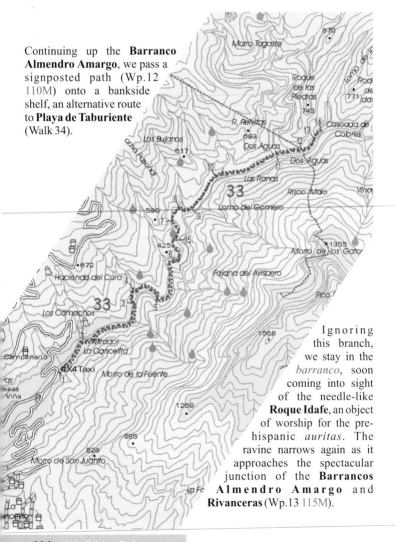

Continuing up the **Barranco Almendro Amargo**, we pass a signposted path (Wp.12 110M) onto a bankside shelf, an alternative route to **Playa de Taburiente** (Walk 34).

Ignoring this branch, we stay in the *barranco*, soon coming into sight of the needle-like **Roque Idafe**, an object of worship for the pre-hispanic *auritas*. The ravine narrows again as it approaches the spectacular junction of the **Barrancos Almendro Amargo** and **Rivanceras** (Wp.13 115M).

The Cascada de Colores

Bearing right into the **Rivanceras**, we splash through the stream and clamber over an outcrop of rock, by-passing a narrow waterchute, to reach the **Cascada de Colores** (Wp.14 125M), which is pretty but not exactly a kaleidoscope, the principal colours being shades of orange and green.

We either return by the same route or, if conditions are good and there's little water in the *barranco*, follow the streambed back to the beginning. The streambed is recommended as it gives an even more impressive perspective on the prodigious cliffs along the ravine. If you don't mind sliding down the occasional bottom-polished rock, this descent is straightforward, except at a small silt dam/waterfall (Wp.15 175M), previously seen on the approach to **Morro de la Era**. Clambering round to the left of the dam, we re-cross the stream via an aqueduct, then follow the canal for twenty-five metres till a cairn-marked way descends back into the streambed. Between Wps.5&3, look out for a couple of faint petroglyphs on a rock to the right.

34 LOS BRECITOS - PLAYA DE TABURIENTE - CASCADA DE LA FONDADA

A walking holiday on La Palma wouldn't be complete without a day in the Caldera, and in this itinerary we combine the easiest route to the **Casas de Taburiente** campsite with a strenuous climb to the most spectacular viewing point inside the crater, the **Mirador de la Cascada Fondada**. 'Playa' de Taburiente is not actually a beach, but a confluence of watercourses where impromptu dams frame shallow plunge-pools. A very slight risk of vertigo en route to the campsite becomes strong on the way up to the *mirador*, though the most vertiginous spots have handrails or railings.

Start early during the summer as the *caldera* really is a cauldron in the afternoon. Don't be deceived by the gentle descent to the *playa*. It's still 300 metres to be climbed at the end of the day.

5*	4¾ H	16 km	** *** and return	⚠	0

*   3 to the *playa*
**   including the return
***   accumulated climb 780 metres – 115 to the *playa*, 365 back, and 300 to the *mirador*

Short Version

To **Playa de Taburiente** (3¼ hours)

Access: by car/4X4T

From **Los Llanos de Aridane** follow the signs for 'Barranco de las Angustias' then take the **Los Brecitos** track to the small parking area at the end, 10.3 kilometres from the bed of the ravine. Ask at the tourist office for 4X4 taxis, or see Appendices at the back of this book.

From the parking area, we take the 'turnstile' path descending behind the mapboard (Wp.1 0M). Ignoring all branches, we follow this well-signposted path all the way to the *playa*, so if you take no great pleasure from being told what you're doing, close the book now and open it again in 80 minutes.

On the descent

The path descends to the first of seven bridges, the fourth of which crosses **Barranco del Ciempies** (Wp.2 10M). Winding along a contour line, we cross **Barranco Cañeras**, after which views open out to the south and we traverse **Lomo de Tenerra** (Wp.3 20M).

After a steady descent, we cross **Barranco de Piedras Redondas** (Wp.4 35M), literally 'round stones', a somewhat inadequate description for the massive lumps of volcanic agglomerate littering the ravine.

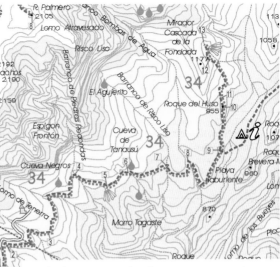

Continuing our steady descent, we pass the **Mirador de Lomo de Tagasaste** (Wp.5 40M) and the **Fuente de la Mula o de la Faya** (Wp.6 45M).

Our next bridge (Wp.7 60M) is over the **Barranco de Risco Liso**, immediately after which we pass a path branching left to petroglyphs. After the bridgeless **Barranco Bombas de Agua** (Wp.8 70M), the sound of trickling water gradually grows to a roar as we glimpse the **Rio Taburiente** way below us and the campsite comes into view. We then descend to a junction just above the **Playa de Taburiente** (Wp.9 80M), where the path to the cascade, signposted 'Hoyo Verde', branches left.

For the short version

We bear right here, crossing the main river and two affluents before climbing to the campsite and information centre.

For the main walk

We turn left, then bear left at a Y-junction for **Hoyo Verde/Cascada de la Fondada**. After zigzagging steadily then steeply up to **Roque del Huso** (Wp.10 100M), we negotiate our first vertiginous stretch helped by a steel handrail and wooden railings, then climb behind the *roque* onto the ridge (Wp.11 110M) we follow to the north. Once again, you can safely ignore the text, so long as you also ignore the occasional minor branch paths and bear in mind there are several vertiginous stretches.

Climbing along the ridge, we pass a very narrow stretch with a chain handrail, then skirt a rocky outcrop, where the path is lined with stumpy posts that are more hazard than help.

After another outcrop and more stumpy posts, we climb steadily alongside a watercourse to a Y-junction (Wp.12 130M). The branch to the right is a shortcut that doesn't really shorten or cut anything, so we bear left on the main path, climbing steadily along the right bank of the watercourse.

We then switch back to the left bank below a couple of bewigged boulders for a final brief climb to the **Mirador Cascada de la Fondada** (Wp.13 140M). The water is meagre, but the fall is immense. We return by the same route.

The Barranco de las Angustias

GPS Waypoints for the walking routes included in **Walk! La Palma** are quoted in Latitude/Longitude for the WGS84 Datum, the default datum for GPS receivers. Before loading waypoints into your GPS unit please read 'Using GPS on La Palma' on page 25.

To input the waypoints into your GPS set the 'location format' to 'hddd° .mm.mmm´ and check that your datum is set to WGS84. While we quote waypoints to four places of decimals, as recorded during our research, you might only be able to input to three places of decimals, depending upon your GPS unit. In this case round the third decimal place to the nearest number; e.g. .0178 would be rounded to .018, while .9224 would be rounded to .922.

The edited GPS Track and Waypoint files for **Walk! La Palma** can be downloaded from our **Personal Navigator Files** (PNFs) CD (version 2.01 onwards) via your PC into your GPS receiver; assuming you have a GPS-PC lead. For more information on our PNFs CD see our websites:-

www.walking.demon.co.uk & www.dwgwalking.co.uk

1 MONTEVERDE: PARED VIEJA - EL PILAR

Wp	N	W
1	28 37.1352	17 49.3428
2	28 36.7674	17 49.0248
3	28 36.6648	17 48.9594
4	28 36.5214	17 48.9150
5	28 36.4734	17 49.0434
6	28 36.4554	17 49.1748
7	28 36.4626	17 49.3386
8	28 36.4584	17 49.4298
9	28 36.4794	17 49.4514
10	28 36.5874	17 49.5924
11	28 36.6036	17 49.7754
12	28 36.6450	17 49.8552
13	28 36.6798	17 49.9128
14	28 36.7128	17 49.9488
15	28 36.8748	17 50.0532
16	28 37.0122	17 49.8774
17	28 37.1034	17 49.5750

2 PISTA DE LOS LOMOS - MONTAÑA DE LA BREÑA - SAN JOSÉ

Wp	N	W
1	28 39.2670	17 49.1514
2	28 39.9928	17 49.2096
3	28 39.9394	17 49.0632
4	28 38.7336	17 49.0374
5	28 38.6322	17 49.1100
6	28 38.4582	17 49.1124
7	28 37.9782	17 49.2468
8	28 37.6152	17 49.2750
9	28 37.2216	17 49.3776
10	28 37.1352	17 49.3488
11	28 37.1418	17 49.2750
12	28 37.2174	17 49.0325
13	28 37.2612	17 48.9125
14	28 37.2564	17 48.6719
15	28 37.4058	17 48.5557
16	28 37.4700	17 48.4356
17	28 37.5288	17 48.3385
18	28 37.7161	17 48.1411
19	28 37.7881	17 48.0144
20	28 37.5727	17 47.4642
21	28 37.7371	17 46.9776
22	28 37.8863	17 46.9884
23	28 38.0909	17 46.9992
24	28 38.2247	17 46.7712
25	28 38.3813	17 46.4975

3 BARRANCO DE LA MADERA

Wp	N	W
1	28 41.6556	17 46.9230
2	28 41.8692	17 47.0730
3	28 42.1242	17 47.2626
4	28 42.3072	17 47.4978
5	28 42.6918	17 48.0156
6	28 42.6768	17 48.1488
7	28 42.8196	17 48.4920
8	28 42.6186	17 48.3186
9	28 42.5508	17 48.1020
10	28 42.4080	17 47.9508
11	28 42.3660	17 47.8500
12	28 42.1152	17 47.5026
13	28 41.9046	17 47.2704
14	28 41.7396	17 47.1156
15	28 41.6916	17 47.0754

4 THE GOOD, THE HIGH, THE LOW & THE BAD

Wp	N	W
1	28 40.4262	17 46.9128
2	28 40.1016	17 47.1168
3	28 39.7980	17 47.2140
4	28 39.5208	17 47.1264
5	28 38.9256	17 47.1846
6	28 38.7096	17 47.0886
7	28 38.5968	17 47.0472
8	28 38.4318	17 46.9944
9	28 38.2812	17 46.9626
10	28 37.8852	17 46.9872
11	28 37.4118	17 47.0226
12	28 37.0404	17 46.9980
13	28 36.8940	17 47.0568
14	28 36.5814	17 47.9590
15	28 36.2796	17 46.9458
16	28 36.0660	17 46.8954
17	28 35.7888	17 46.9254
18	28 35.4108	17 46.9974
19	28 35.3490	17 47.1312
20	28 35.0154	17 47.2266
21	28 34.9956	17 46.9956
22	28 34.9884	17 46.8846
23	28 34.5198	17 46.8222
24	28 34.4010	17 46.7220

5 FUENTES DE LAS BREÑAS

Wp	N	W
1	28 39.7578	17 47.2992
2	28 39.7164	17 47.4558
3	28 39.8526	17 47.8680
4	28 39.8676	17 48.0876
5	28 39.8784	17 48.2202
6	28 39.8394	17 48.1980
7	28 39.8814	17 48.2604
8	28 39.7506	17 48.2694
9	28 39.6960	17 48.2556
10	28 39.6054	17 48.1014
11	28 39.4752	17 48.1140
12	28 39.3462	17 48.0840
13	28 39.2352	17 48.1032
14	28 39.1692	17 48.2052
15	28 39.1362	17 48.1956
16	28 39.0882	17 48.2358
17	28 39.0750	17 47.9820
18	28 39.0294	17 47.9772
19	28 38.9376	17 47.9532
20	28 38.9190	17 47.8956
21	28 39.0606	17 47.5062
22	28 39.3306	17 47.4024

6 CUMBRE NUEVA LOOP

Wp	N	W
1	28 39.2280	17 51.2088
2	28 39.6774	17 51.0954
3	28 39.7776	17 50.4678
4	28 39.9960	17 50.0994
5	28 40.1082	17 49.6302
6	28 36.8814	17 50.0568
7	28 36.8442	17 50.1990
8	28 37.2048	17 50.5488
9	28 37.3056	17 50.5710
10	28 37.3788	17 50.6898
11	28 37.5018	17 50.7582
12	28 37.9368	17 50.7354
13	28 38.0046	17 50.7552
14	28 38.0622	17 50.7804
15	28 38.2374	17 50.8626
16	28 38.3586	17 50.8974
17	28 38.6190	17 51.0990
18	28 38.8926	17 51.2214
19	28 39.1374	17 51.4398

7 PICO BIRIGOYO

Wp	N	W
1	28 36.8424	17 50.1924
2	28 36.7548	17 50.1522
3	28 36.6234	17 50.2158
4	28 36.5820	17 50.3952
5	28 36.3714	17 50.6052
6	28 36.3018	17 50.6046
7	28 36.2784	17 50.6646
8	28 36.1518	17 50.6256
9	28 36.2946	17 50.4546
10	28 36.5232	17 50.2008
11	28 36.5664	17 50.1360

8 RUTA DE LOS VOLCANOS

Wp	N	W
1	28 36.8424	17 50.1924
2	28 36.7548	17 50.1522
3	28 36.6234	17 50.2158
4	28 36.5820	17 50.3952
5	28 36.3714	17 50.6052
6	28 36.1948	17 50.7840
7	28 35.8110	17 50.5644
8	28 35.2944	17 50.3898
9	28 35.2452	17 50.2638
10	28 35.0148	17 50.2518
11	28 34.6128	17 50.3454
12	28 34.2066	17 50.3682
13	28 34.1358	17 50.3556
14	28 33.9246	17 50.2776
15	28 33.7584	17 50.2116
16	28 32.8728	17 50.3718
17	28 32.6130	17 50.3898
18	28 32.4210	17 50.3634
19	28 32.1612	17 50.5620
20	28 31.6362	17 50.3976
21	28 31.5738	17 50.2866
22	28 31.1334	17 50.0880
23	28 30.6192	17 50.3568
24	28 30.2994	17 50.5692
25	28 29.9892	17 50.8272
26	28 29.7156	17 50.6964

9 VOLCÁN MARTÍN

Wp	N	W
1	28 31.4718	17 50.9358
2	28 31.6260	17 50.8512
3	28 32.0520	17 50.6502
4	28 32.0862	17 50.5668
5	28 32.1594	17 50.5632
6	28 32.2860	17 50.4912
7	28 32.4204	17 50.3616
8	28 32.1864	17 50.4144
9	28 32.0112	17 50.5680
10	28 31.7634	17 50.3748
11	28 31.6410	17 50.3976
12	28 31.5462	17 50.4540
13	28 31.3290	17 50.6598
14	28 31.5618	17 50.8230

9A Alt.

Wp	N	W
1	28 31.1548	17 49.9905
2	28 31.1224	17 50.0781
3	28 31.4998	17 50.2563
4	28 31.6996	17 50.0925
5	28 31.7734	17 49.8681
6	28 32.5558	17 49.6209

10 THE SOUTHERN VOLCANOES

Wp	N	W
1	28 28.5690	17 51.1458
2	28 28.6674	17 51.2616
3	28 28.8618	17 51.3588
4	28 28.8234	17 51.1812
5	28 29.1768	17 51.1668
6	28 29.1894	17 50.9154
7	28 28.9728	17 51.0876
8	28 29.1792	17 50.8752
9	28 29.0496	17 50.8026
10	28 28.6956	17 50.7132
11	28 28.4772	17 51.0408
12	28 28.3158	17 51.1140

11 COLADAS DE SAN JUAN

Wp	N	W
1	28 36.1212	17 52.8588
2	28 36.3180	17 52.7574
3	28 36.3234	17 52.6320
4	28 36.3216	17 52.4112
5	28 36.3714	17 52.1250
6	28 36.3636	17 51.9876
7	28 36.4782	17 52.0464
8	28 36.4206	17 51.8646
9	28 36.4074	17 51.7968
10	28 36.3606	17 51.7176
11	28 36.2688	17 51.6018
12	28 36.2190	17 51.5184
13	28 36.0582	17 51.6468
14	28 35.9892	17 51.6582
15	28 35.9376	17 51.7116
16	28 35.9472	17 51.9396
17	28 35.8530	17 52.1508
18	28 36.1140	17 52.5858

12 MIRADOR DEL TIME - TAZACORTE

Wp	N	W
1	28 39.8310	17 56.5542
2	28 39.5160	17 56.6598
3	28 39.3468	17 56.8758
4	28 39.1824	17 56.9568
5	28 39.1938	17 56.8452
6	28 39.1224	17 56.8632
7	28 39.0984	17 56.7258

13 TINIZARA - EL JESÚS

Wp	N	E
1	28 44.6260	17 58.1019
2	28 44.4190	17 58.1331
3	28 44.2708	17 58.1871
4	28 44.1610	17 58.2477
5	28 43.9954	17 58.1769
6	28 43.7680	17 58.1175
7	28 43.7218	17 58.0605
8	28 43.6474	17 57.9459
9	28 43.5208	17 57.8439
10	28 43.4512	17 57.6051
11	28 43.2922	17 57.5193
12	28 43.0570	17 57.5330
13	28 42.9490	17 57.5282
14	28 42.7258	17 57.2480
15	28 42.4990	17 57.1424
16	28 42.4348	17 57.0542
17	28 42.3766	17 56.9984
18	28 42.3328	17 57.1160
19	28 42.3154	17 57.1568
20	28 42.1522	17 57.2408
21	28 42.2188	17 57.1268

14 RISCO DE LAS PAREDITAS

Wp	N	W
1	28 42.3462	17 55.9566
2	28 42.2502	17 55.7154
3	28 42.2898	17 55.5222
4	28 42.3234	17 55.1580
5	28 42.2922	17 54.9672
6	28 42.0180	17 55.1160
7	28 41.9274	17 55.3314
8	28 41.7972	17 55.4202
9	28 41.7396	17 55.4490
10	28 41.5638	17 55.4520
11	28 41.4450	17 55.5906
12	28 41.3244	17 55.6362
13	28 41.5674	17 55.6476
14	28 41.6220	17 55.8060
15	28 41.7192	17 55.8534
16	28 41.7840	17 55.9122
17	28 42.0306	17 55.9860
18	28 42.0492	17 55.9974
19	28 42.1788	17 56.0274

15 CUEVAS DE BURACAS

Wp	N	W
1	28 46.8354	17 57.7830
2	28 46.8222	17 57.8706
3	28 46.8798	17 57.9822
4	28 47.0694	17 58.1580
5	28 47.1438	17 58.3080
6	28 47.1942	17 58.3632
7	28 47.2956	17 58.3830
8	28 47.3808	17 58.4322
9	28 47.5248	17 58.5180
10	28 47.5656	17 58.6368
11	28 47.5818	17 58.6116
12	28 47.5728	17 58.5300
13	28 47.6628	17 58.5276
14	28 47.5518	17 58.3650

16 HOYA GRANDE: EL PINAR DE GARAFÍA

Wp	N	W
1	28 47.6448	17 55.1700
2	28 47.6754	17 55.0266
3	28 47.7594	17 54.9462
4	28 47.7516	17 54.5898
5	28 48.0990	17 54.1530
6	28 47.7696	17 54.2394
7	28 47.5422	17 54.2136
8	28 47.4774	17 54.3630
9	28 47.3790	17 54.5586
10	28 47.3622	17 54.6714
11	28 47.4804	17 54.7170

17 SANTO DOMINGO

Wp	N	W
1	28 48.3558	17 55.4753
2	28 48.4380	17 55.6266
3	28 48.6474	17 55.7442
4	28 48.7878	17 55.7730
5	28 49.1202	17 55.9608
6	28 49.4130	17 56.1342
7	28 49.5444	17 56.1642
8	28 49.7664	17 55.9524
9	28 50.3796	17 56.0580
10	28 50.2236	17 56.2686
11	28 49.9422	17 56.5926
12	28 49.8456	17 56.6688

18 BARRANCO FAGUNDO

Wp	N	W
1	28 50.0124	17 52.6397
2	28 50.1648	17 52.6679
3	28 50.0994	17 52.8498
4	28 50.1924	17 52.8612
5	28 50.2614	17 53.0112
6	28 50.0946	17 53.0994

19 CALDERA DE AGUA 1

Wp	N	W
1	28 48.1794	17 52.8078
2	28 48.1374	17 52.9794
3	28 48.1050	17 53.2890
4	28 47.9730	17 53.4366
5	28 47.9616	17 53.6382
6	28 47.9346	17 53.7108
7	28 47.9172	17 53.8506
8	28 48.0096	17 53.9472
9	28 48.0900	17 54.0564
10	28 48.2382	17 54.1326
11	28 48.3060	17 54.1812
12	28 48.3738	17 54.3594
13	28 48.4320	17 54.4134
14	28 48.5442	17 54.4314
15	28 48.5514	17 54.4488
16	28 48.7524	17 54.4890
17	28 48.8472	17 54.4080
18	28 48.8322	17 54.4470
19	28 48.9480	17 54.5298
20	28 48.9456	17 54.5862
21	28 48.9006	17 54.6582
22	28 48.8256	17 54.8856
23	28 48.8004	17 54.8016
24	28 48.7032	17 54.6696
25	28 48.4812	17 54.5244

20 CALDERA DE AGUA 11

Wp	N	W
1	28 48.3786	17 54.3738
2	28 48.4872	17 54.2688
3	28 48.6492	17 54.0504
4	28 48.7404	17 53.8638
5	28 48.9534	17 53.8350
6	28 49.3062	17 53.7126
7	28 49.3838	17 53.8890
8	28 49.3614	17 54.1122
9	28 49.2438	17 54.1608
10	28 49.1418	17 54.2088
11	28 48.8760	17 54.4512
12	28 48.8184	17 54.4524
13	28 48.6522	17 54.4428
14	28 48.4254	17 54.4254

21
2 SHORT WALKS IN THE NORTH:

(a) BARRANCO DE LOS HOMBRES

Wp	N	W
1	28 48.1830	17 52.6908
2	28 47.9400	17 52.7238
3	28 47.9154	17 52.5906
4	28 47.8002	17 52.5588
5	28 47.6958	17 52.4466
6	28 47.4594	17 52.3014
7	28 47.7330	17 52.0968
8	28 48.2262	17 52.2006

(b) MONTAÑA DE LAS VARAS

Wp	N	W
1	28 49.0481	17 54.7568
2	28 49.0919	17 54.5348
3	28 49.1609	17 54.3056
4	28 49.2479	17 54.2474
5	28 49.4783	17 54.3392
6	28 49.5575	17 54.5054
7	28 49.6637	17 54.4400

22
BARLOVENTO - GALLEGOS

Wp	N	W
1	28 49.5696	17 48.3570
2	28 49.6158	17 48.6876
3	28 49.6968	17 48.7506
4	28 49.7178	17 48.9702
5	28 49.6722	17 49.1616
6	28 49.6056	17 49.2840
7	28 49.6002	17 49.3704
8	28 49.4724	17 49.4562
9	28 49.5126	17 49.5150
10	28 49.6638	17 49.6548
11	28 49.6284	17 49.7346
12	28 49.5450	17 49.8204
13	28 49.6212	17 49.9344
14	28 49.4970	17 50.0574
15	28 49.5798	17 50.1420
16	28 49.6806	17 50.2128
17	28 49.7400	17 50.2920

23
MOTAÑA DEL POZO

Wp	N	W
1	28 49.5696	17 48.3570
2	28 49.6158	17 48.6876
3	28 49.6968	17 48.7506
4	28 49.7178	17 48.9702
5	28 49.6722	17 49.1616
6	28 49.6056	17 49.2840
7	28 49.6002	17 49.3704
8	28 49.4724	17 49.4562
9	28 49.5126	17 49.5150
10	28 49.6638	17 49.6548
11	28 49.6284	17 49.7346
12	28 49.5006	17 49.6260
13	28 49.1994	17 49.2852
14	28 48.9936	17 49.1310
15	28 49.0284	17 49.0524
16	28 48.9384	17 49.0314
17	28 49.0224	17 48.9642
18	28 49.1784	17 48.8946
19	28 49.0818	17 48.5922
20	28 49.1358	17 48.4914

24
BARLOVENTO - LOS SAUCES via MIRADOR DE LA BARANDA

Wp	N	W
1	28 49.5324	17 48.3468
2	28 49.1388	17 48.4878
3	28 48.8226	17 48.5418
4	28 48.8286	17 48.2340
5	28 48.7302	17 48.2130
6	28 48.4938	17 48.3162
7	28 48.4242	17 48.4668
8	28 48.2784	17 48.5304
9	28 48.1740	17 48.5352
10	28 48.0738	17 48.6942
11	28 48.0180	17 48.7674
12	28 47.8176	17 48.8550
13	28 47.8704	17 48.2646
14	28 47.8002	17 48.0246
15	28 47.7810	17 47.8320
16	28 48.0654	17 47.3004
17	28 48.2652	17 46.4382

27
THE DEVIL'S WALL

Wp	N	W
1	28 45.4230	17 51.3426
2	28 45.3900	17 51.3564
3	28 45.2550	17 51.2106
4	28 45.5706	17 51.6228
5	28 45.6660	17 52.0404
6	28 45.5976	17 52.1874
7	28 45.5820	17 52.3128
8	28 45.7158	17 52.4808

28
ROQUE PALMERO

Wp	N	W
1	28 45.1326	17 53.4180
2	28 44.9808	17 53.6274
3	28 44.8764	17 53.6766
4	28 44.6910	17 53.8428
5	28 44.5596	17 53.9652
6	28 44.4552	17 54.0042
7	28 44.3142	17 54.0264
8	28 44.2596	17 53.8962

29
PICO DE LA CRUZ - PICO DE LA NIEVE

Wp	N	W
1	28 45.4230	17 51.3426
2	28 45.2550	17 51.2106
3	28 44.9796	17 50.7486
4	28 44.9676	17 50.7114
5	28 44.8278	17 50.4462
6	28 44.6862	17 50.2890
7	28 44.5740	17 50.2068
8	28 44.1078	17 50.1342
9	28 44.0232	17 50.1276
10	28 43.7760	17 50.1234

30
PICO DE LA NIEVE

Wp	N	W
1	28 43.9914	17 49.3440
2	28 43.9788	17 49.7394
3	28 43.8546	17 49.8096
4	28 43.8114	17 49.8408
5	28 43.7316	17 50.1324
6	28 43.7760	17 50.1240
7	28 43.5990	17 50.0940
8	28 43.8756	17 49.8330

31
LA CUMBRECITA: MIRADORS DE LA CHOZA & DE LOS ROQUES + CANAL to GALERÍA DE ARIDANE

Wp	N	W
1	28 41.8734	17 51.3894
2	28 41.9352	17 51.8124
3	28 42.0276	17 51.8442
4	28 41.8632	17 51.6384
5	28 41.8938	17 51.5058
6	28 41.9718	17 51.4110
7	28 41.9994	17 51.4392
8	28 41.9412	17 51.3606
9	28 42.0612	17 51.3348
10	28 42.4260	17 51.1182

32

PICO BEJENADO

Wp	N	W
1	28 40.6818	17 51.2610
2	28 40.9782	17 51.7146
3	28 41.0856	17 51.7254
4	28 41.1936	17 51.7122
5	28 41.3184	17 52.0164
6	28 41.3484	17 52.2042
7	28 41.4348	17 52.4274
8	28 41.5494	17 52.6056

33

BARRANCO DE LOS ANGUSTIAS & CASCADA DE LOS COLORES

Wp	N	W
1	28 41.1990	17 54.5232
2	28 41.3790	17 54.3372
3	28 41.5692	17 54.0366
4	28 41.6538	17 54.0172
5	28 41.6352	17 53.8548
6	28 41.8080	17 53.7072
7	28 42.0456	17 53.7138
8	28 42.1164	17 53.6658
9	28 42.1368	17 53.5920
10	28 42.2766	17 53.4786
11	28 42.3978	17 53.0172
12	28 42.4506	17 52.8606
13	28 42.5226	17 52.7616
14	28 42.6000	17 52.6248
15	28 41.9262	17 53.7126

34

LOS BRECITOS - PLAYA DE TABURIENTE - CASCADA DE FONDADA

Wp	N	W
1	28 42.6960	17 54.0384
2	28 42.9552	17 54.0726
3	28 43.0176	17 53.7954
4	28 43.3344	17 53.5974
5	28 43.2702	17 53.3676
6	28 43.3524	17 53.2182
7	28 43.4130	17 52.9740
8	28 43.4274	17 52.7874
9	28 43.4952	17 52.5864
10	28 43.7106	17 52.5762
11	28 43.7556	17 52.5804
12	28 44.0190	17 52.6710
13	28 44.1228	17 52.6806

GLOSSARY

This glossary contains Spanish words found in the text (shown in *italics*),
plus other local words that you may encounter.

a

abandonado — abandoned, in poor repair
abierto — open
acampamiento — camping
acequia — water channel
aeropuerto — airport
agua — water
agua no potable — water (not drinkable)
agua potable — drinking water
alto — high
aparcamiento — parking
área recreativa — official picnic spot, usually with barbecues, toilets, water taps
arroyo — stream
ayuntamiento — town hall

b

bajo — low
barranco — ravine
bocadillo — bread roll
bodegón — inn
bosque — wood
cabezo — peak, summit

c

cabra — goat
cabrera — goatherd
calle — street
camí — path or way
camino — trail, path, track
camino particular — private road
camino real — old donkey trail (lit. royal road)
carretera — main road
casa — house
casa forestal — forestry house
casa rural — country house accommodation to let
cascada — waterfall
caserío — hamlet, village
cementario — cemetry
centro salud — health centre
cerrado — closed

cerveza — beer
charco — literally a puddle, commonly used for a watering hole (inland), or natural/semi natural coastal swimming pool
choza — shelter
clinica — clinic, hospital
colegio — college, school
comida — food
cordillera — mountain range
correos — post office
cortijo — farmstead
costa — coast
coto privado de caza — private hunting area
Cruz Roja — Red Cross (medical aid)
cuesta — slope
cueva — cave
cumbre — summit

d

degollado — pass
derecha — right (direction)
desprendimiento — landslide
drago — 'Dragon' Tree

e

embalse — reservoir
ermita — chapel
Espacio Naturaleza Protegido — protected area of natural beauty
estación de autobus/ guagua — bus station

f

farmacia — chemist
faro — lighthouse
fiesta — holiday, celebration
finca — farm, country house
fuente — spring or source

g

galeria — canalisation pipe

gasolinera	petrol station
guagua	bus
guanche	original Canary Islands inhabitants
Guardia Civil	police
guia	guide

h

hostal	hostel, accommodation
hoya	depression (geological)
iglesia	church

i

información	information
isla	island
izquierda	left (direction)

l

laurisilva	ancient laurel forest
lavadero	laundry area (usually communal)
librería	bookshop
llano	plain
lluvioso	rainy
lomo	broad-backed ridge or spur dividing two valleys or ravines

m

malpais	'bad lands' wild, barren countryside
mapa	map
mercado	market
mirador	lookout/viewing point
montaña	mountain

n

nublado	cloudy
nueva/o	new

o

oficina de turismo	tourist office

p

peligroso	danger
pensión	guesthouse
pescado	fish
pico	peak
picón	black volcanic rock/sand
piscina	swimming pool
pista	dirt road/track

pista (forestal)	forest road/track
playa	beach
plaza	square
policia	police
pozo	well
prohibido el paso	no entry
puente	bridge
puerto	port, mountain pass

r

refugio	refuge, shelter
río	river, stream
risco	crag or cliff
roque	(a) lava fill exposed by erosion to form a broad, blunt pinnacle (b) rock
ruta	route

s

salida	exit
senda	path, track
sendero	foot path
sierra	mountain range
sin salida	no through road/route
sirocco	hot, dust-laden wind from Africa

t

tapas	bar snacks
tienda	shop
tipico	traditional bar/eating place
tormentoso	stormy
torre	tower
torrente	stream
tubería	water pipe

v

valle	valley
vega	meadow
ventoso	windy
vereda	path, lane
vieja/o	old

z

zona recreativa	recreation area

Please note:

Telephone numbers are shown in red, and fax numbers in blue, and we show the entire number you need to dial from outside Spain. From within Spain, omit the 00 34. Websites and email addresses are shown in green.

TOURIST OFFICE INFORMATION

Tourist Information Offices offer a number of give-away leaflets worth getting hold of. Most are produced by the Patronato de Turismo and carry the legend, 'La Palma - la isla bonita' (the beautiful island).
The main office is at:

> Calle O'Daly 22, Santa Cruz La Palma
> 00 34 922 412106
> 00 34 922 412106/423347
> www.lapalmaturismo.com
> informacion@lapalmaturismo.com

Other Tourist Information Offices
- Centro de Visitantes, El Paso, at 23.9km on the LP2 east-west road
- Avda. Doctor Fleming, Los Llanos de Aridane
- Airport

Look for these freebies in the Tourist Offices (check you've picked up the English language version):

Free Maps

La Palma - La Isla Bonita Basic, small island map plus rough sketch maps of **Santa Cruz de La Palma** and **Los Llanos de Aridane**

Caldera de Taburiente Sketch map leaflet of the **Caldera**.

Free Booklets & Magazines

Hiking Guide Seven routes are described, but the tiny, basic map is of little use.
A Historical and Artistic Guide to Santa Cruz de la Palma
Typical Cuisine of La Palma
The Benahoaritas - the ancient inhabitants of La Palma
Leisure Activities Guide
CLIP Magazine Quarterly information magazine - in Spanish but with useful addresses, opening hours, bus times etc.
La Palma Magazine Tri-lingual give-away, heavy on illustrations, light on information.

MAPS

Two Spanish organisations publish the closest equivalents to traditional Ordnance Survey style maps. They are:-

Centro Nacional de Información Geográfica
Oficina Central, Monte Esquinza, 41
28010 Madrid, Spain
00 34 91 5979453   00 34 91 5532913
www.cnig.es   consulta@cnig.es

Servicio Geográfico del Ejército
Dario Gazapo, 8
28024 Madrid, Spain
00 34 91 7115043   00 34 91 7115033

La Palma Tour & Trail Super-Durable 1:40,000 scale Map (Pub.
Discovery Walking Guides Ltd.) £7.99 **ISBN 1-904946-07-0**
Printed on tough Polyart material, virtually tear proof and waterproof, this
companion publication is the recommended map.

La Palma 1:50,000 scale Map (Pub. Freytag & Berndt) **ISBN 3-850842-59-2**
Despite its description as a road map, short on road numbers.

La Palma 1:50,000 scale Map (Pub. Kompass)
More detailed than Freytag & Berndt.

BOOKS

Walking in the Canary Islands: 1 West by Paddy Dillon (Pub.
Cicerone) £12.00 **ISBN 1-852843-65-9**
It's hardly surprising that a book attempting to cover 4 very different islands
struggles to do justice to any one of them. Only about one seventh of this book
(36 pages) deals specifically with La Palma, offering just 8 routes. Maps are
basic and timings on the routes non-existent - not good value in our opinion -
and why carry 220 irrelevant pages around with you?

Landscapes of La Palma and El Hierro by Noel Rochford
2002) (Pub. Sunflower Books) £10.99 **ISBN 1-856912-14-0**
Well known series, but lumping these two very different islands together isn't
very useful. Walk descriptions vary in reliability and detail.

La Palma: The Finest Valley and Mountain Walks (Rother
Walking Guide)
Klaus Wolfsperger, Tony Pearson (Pub. Bergverlag Rother) £8.99 **ISBN 3-763348-08-5**
Loses something in the translation from the original German perhaps.

Lonely Planet Canary Islands by Sarah Andrews, Chris Andrews,
Sally O'Brien (Pub. Lonely Planet Publications) £11.99 **ISBN 1-740593-74-X**
Useful background reading from this respected publisher.

Flores Silvestres de las Islas Canarias by David & Zoe Bramwell
(Pub. Editorial Rueda, Aptdo de Correos 43.001, Porto Cristo 13,

Alcorcon, Madrid, Spain)
This is the serious plantperson's must-have publication. This impressive and comprehensive tome, published in Spanish, might be available on the island. There was an English translation published in 2001 £35 **ISBN 8-472071-29-4** which you may find via www.amazon.co.uk

 Los Volcanes de las Islas Canarias (1) by Araña, Vicente and Carracedo (Pub. Editorial Rueda, address as above)
In Spanish only, but if you're an enthusiast, it's essential.

WEBSITES

General websites on the Canaries

www.candir.com
www.canary-guide.com
www.canary-islands.com
www.spaintour.com/canarias.htm
www.gobcan.es
www.fredolsen.es

Websites specific to La Palma

www.ecoturismocanarias.com
www.infoisla.org
www.infolapalma.com
www.islabonita.com
www.lapalmaturismo.com
www.lapalma-magazin.info
www.mma.es/parques/lared/caldera
www.lapalmabiosfera.com
www.malvasiadelapalma.com

ACCOMMODATION

Since we were camping, the following addresses come from other publications and are not personal recommendations.

 In/around Santa Cruz

Pension Arrocha	00 34 922 411117
Pension Bahia	00 34 922 411846
Pension La Cubana	00 34 922 411354
Pension Canarias	00 34 922 413182
Apartamentos La Fuente	00 34 922 415636
Apartamentos Montecristo	00 34 922 415636
Apartamentos Rocamar	00 34 922 411946
Hotel Maritimo	00 34 922 420222
Hotel Avenida	00 34 922 420624
Parador	00 34 922 435828

Chipi-Chipi
(see restaurants below)   www.web-glass.com/up/chipichipi.htm

 Breña Baja
Hacienda San Jorge   00 34 922 181066 00 34 922 434528
                                www.hsanjorge.com

 In/around Fuencaliente

Pension Los Volcanes   00 34 922 441464
Pension Central   00 34 922 444018
Pension Imperial   00 34 922 444018

 In/around Los Llanos de Aridane

Pension El Time   00 34 922 460907
Pension Rocha   00 34 922 460157
Hotel Eden   00 34 922 460104
Hotel Valle de Aridane   00 34 922 462600 00 34 922 401019
                                  www.hotelvallearidane.com
Apartamentos Dona Paquita   00 34 922 402000 00 34 922 460948
                                  paquita@lapalma.com
Apartamentos Luz y Mar   00 34 922 408163
Apartamentos Martin   00 34 922 408046
Apartamentos El Patio   00 34 922 461500 00 34 922 461500
                                  www.elpatio-lapalma.com

 El Paso
La Palma Jardin   00 34 922 463567   00 34 922 461316
                                  www.lapalmajardin.com

 In the North

Los Sauces
Pension Argeo   00 34 922 450239
Pension El Drago   00 34 922 450121

 Barlovento

Apartamentos La Fajana   00 34 922 413761
Hotel La Palma Romantica   00 34 922 186221

 Tazacorte
Atlantis Apartamentos   00 34 922 462600   00 34 922 401019
                                  atlantis@atlantis-lapalma.com

Casas Rurales (renovated country cottages)

www.infolapalma.com/islabonita

CAMPSITES & CAMPING INFORMATION

 Caldera de Taburiente   00 34 922 497277
Centro de Visitantes
Carretera General de Padrón
38750 El Paso

 La Laguna de Barlovento   00 34 922 696023
Oficina de Información

 Medio Ambiente   00 34 922 411583
Avenida Los Indianos 20-2°
38770 Santa Cruz de La Palma

- for camping at **El Pilar** and **Fuencaliente** refuges.

 Hacienda San Antonio del Monte   00 34 922 400444
38787 Santo Domingo (Garafía)

RESTAURANTS

Restaurants in/around **Santa Cruz**:

El Encuentro (Plaza de la Alameda) for good *arepas* and an ideal spot to while away the evening watching the world go by

Restaurante Canarias (Avenida Maritima) serves good, reasonably priced fish and meat dishes

La Placeta (Placeta de Borrero) is more up-market, but worth the extra money

Restaurante Chipi-Chipi (Carretera de las Nieves) is said to be the best value restaurant on the island, which is debatable, but indisputable is the high quality of the food and the uniqueness of the décor, a kind of modernist grotto with individual dining 'caves'

Las Tres Chimeneas (Buenavista de Arriba) is reputedly the absolute best, though it has a serious competitor in the

Parador, which has eschewed the usual bland 'international' menu in favour of a genuinely original take on La Palman cuisine.

This is not an exhaustive survey, but several obvious routes stand out. Running clockwise from Santa Cruz:

A The PR2.2 to **Santuario de las Nieves**

B **Pista de los Lomos** (see Walk 2)

C **Barranco de la Madera** (Walk 3) to the end of the dirt track

D **Pista Hilera de la Cumbre** along the **Cumbre Nueva** (see Walk 6)

E **Pista del Este** (also known as **El Cabrito**) along the eastern flank of the **Cumbre Vieja** (see Walks 1, 8&9)

F **Pista del Oeste** along the western flank of the **Cumbre Vieja** (see Walks 8&9)

G **Malpais – Montaña de Azufre**

H **Monte de Luna – El Poris – Tigalate**

I The **Teneguia** dirt track and **El Faro** (see Walk 10)

J **El Paso Centro de Visitantes - La Cumbrecita** LP202

K The road & track from **Llanos de Aridane** to the **Mirador de la Cancelita**

L The **Los Brecitos** *pista forestal* from **Llanos de Aridane**

M A German mountain-bike club has left stickers on part of the route descending from **Torre del Time** to the **Mirador del Time Bar/Restaurante** (whether this is legal let alone desirable, I have no idea)

N **Tinizara – Refugio de Tinizara – Torre del Time – El Pinar – El Jesús**

O **Tinizara – Briestas** LP115

P **La Traviesa** between **Briestas** and **El Jesús**

Q **Las Tricias – Santo Domingo** LP114

R Walk 16

(S)	The short version of Walk 17
(T)	Walks 21 **(a)** & **(b)**
(U)	**Pista Machin** between the **El Tablado** turn-off and **Puntagorda**
(V)	**Barlovento** - **Roque del Faro** via **Las Mimbreras** LP111 (a must for motorists and cyclists alike, the latter should do it west to east for a longer descent)
(W)	The **Nacimientos de Marcos y Cordero** *pista forestal* from **Las Lomadas** to **Casa del Monte** (see Walk 25)
(X)	**Pista de los Montes de Galga** (see Walk 26)
(Y)	The track descending east, down to **Puntallana**, a few hundred metres north of the **Pico de las Nieves** turn-off.

Mountain Biking (Hiring and touring)

Club Ciclista La Palma   00 34 922 408355 00 34 922 408355
Avenida Cruz Roja, 3, Puerto Naos
and
Calle San Antonio, 88, Breña Baja 00 34 922 434309 00 34 922 434309
                                                www.bike-station.de

Bike'n Fun   00 34 922 401927 00 34 922 401927
Calvo Sotelo, 20
Los Llanos de Aridane   www.bikefun.de

Bici-Tour, Los Cancajos
                                                www.bicitour.es

Horse Riding

Centro Hípico la Vaquera   629 824551
Carretera El Pinar, km 4.6
San Isidro, Breña Baja

Cuadra Taburiente   00 34 922 402545
Carretera El Cumbre, 24, El Paso

Circulo Hípico Manivasán   00 34 922486312   00 34 922 486312
Camino Pepe Jiménez, 15, El Paso (in front of La Cascada restaurant)

Paseos a Caballo   659 157661
Based in the north (Garafía)

Sociedad Hípica Miranda La Palma
Camino San Miguel, Breña Alta   00 34 922 437696

Parachuting/Paragliding

Escuela Parapente Palmasur   00 34 922 444549 00 34 922 444549
Calle la Cruz, 2, Los Quemados
Fuencaliente   www.mipaginade/parapentepalmasur

Asociación Deportiva Palmaclub 00 34 922 408172 00 34 922 408121
Calle Mauricio Duque Camacho, 21
Puerto Naos   palmaclub@airtel.net

Caving

Grupo Espeleología Benisahare 00 34 922 181008
Contact Paco Govantes
(only Spanish spoken)   fgovmor@gobiernodecanarias.org

Scuba Diving

Club Atlantic 28   00 34 922 444047 00 34 922 444047
Carretera General Fuencaliente, 106
Los Canarios   www.atlantic28.de

la Palma Diving Centre   00 34 922 181393 00 34 922181393
Cancajos Centro Commercial
Breña Baja, Los Cancajos beach   www.la-palma-tauchen.de

Tauchpartner La Palma s.l.   00 34 922 408139 00 34 922 401493
Carretera General
Puerto Naos - El Remo, 438   www.la-palma.de/tauchpartner

Club La Palma Sub   00 34 922420355 00 34 922 420355
Barranco del Carmen, 9
Santa Cruz de La Palma

Boat Trips

Excursiones Marítimas Agamenón
Puerto de Tazacorte

Charter María s.l. 'Fancy 11' 00 34 922 401256 00 34 922 406057
                                   www.lp-b.com/fancy

Ask in the **Tourist Information Office** for precise directions and current opening hours.

Casa Museo del Vino (Wine Museum)
Las Manchas (next to La Glorieta Square)
Privately run wine making, tasting, buying. Exhibition of photos of the 1949 eruption of the San Juan volcano.

Centro Visitantes Volcanes Fuencaliente (Volcano Visitors' Centre)
Fuencaliente
Local authority run exhibition centring on the San Antonio volcano, and café.

Taller de Seda Artesanía (Silk Workshop)
Las Hilanderas, El Paso
Local authority run demonstrations and museum and sale of products

Museo Etnográfico Villa de Garafía
Casa de la Cultura, Santo Domingo
Local authority museum of local natural history.

Molino Hidráulico El Regente (Hydraulic Windmill)
Los Molinos, San Andrés
Gofio windmill, now a local authority run flour museum and handicraft centre.

Museo Naval (Maritime Museum)
Plaza de la Alameda, Santa Cruz de La Palma
Reproduction of Columbus' vessel 'Santa María', now housing a cartography exhibition.

Museo Insular (Island Museum)
Plaza de San Francisco, Santa Cruz de La Palma
The Island Government runs this museum of natural sciences, arts and archaeology.

Museo del Plátano (Banana Museum)
Camino San Antonio, El Charco, Tazacorte

Parque Botánico y Faunístico 'Maroparque'
La Cuesta, 28, Breña Alta
Zoo, aquarium and flora collections plus the usual shop, bar, café

Parque Paraíso de las Aves   www.la-palma-de/vogelpark
Panadera, 16, El Paso
Bird, flora and fauna park, including endangered species.

TAXIS

Auto-Taxi Martín   629 980747/609 215405 639/384555
24 hour service
Serves **Caldera de Taburiente**, **Refugio El Pilar**, **Los Tilos**, **Roque de los Muchachos**, **Pico de la Nieve** (Walks 8, 25, 33, 34)

Taxi 4x4 daily 08.30 - 13.00   629 161819/609 539381
To the source of **Las Angustias** (Walk 33)

Pepe's 4x4 Taxi   649 945481/616 418847/616 418848
and
Taxi 4x4 (Rural Taxis)   922 450928
From **Los Tilos** to **Casa del Monte** (Walk 25)

 **EMERGENCIES**

Phone 211 (equivalent of 999)

BUS TIMETABLES

Please note that Transportes Insular La Palma's timetables are subject to change. Ask in tourist offices or the bus station in **Santa Cruz de La Palma** for current times.

L1 SANTA CRUZ DE LA PALMA - LOS LLANOS DE ARIDANE via LA CUMBRE

Departures from

S. C. de La Palma	Los Llanos de Aridane
05.00	
06.15*	06.30*
07.15	07.30
08.15*	08.30*
09.15	09.30
10.15*	10.30*
11.15	11.30
12.15*	12.30*
13.15	13.30
14.15*	14.30*
15.15	15.30
16.15*	16.30*
17.15	17.30
18.15*	18.30*
19.15	19.30
20.15*	20.30*
21.45	21.30

L1A LOS LLANOS DE ARIDANE - EL PASO

Departures from

Los Llanos de Aridane	El Paso
05.00	
06.30*	07.00
07.30	08.00
08.30*	09.00*
09.00*	09.30*
09.30	10.00
10.00*	10.30*
10.30*	11.00*
11.00*	11.30*
11.30	12.00
12.00*	12.30*
12.30*	13.00*
13.00*	13.30*
13.30	14.00
14.00*	14.30*
14.30*	15.00*
15.30	16.00
16.30*	17.00*
17.30	18.00
18.30*	19.00*
19.30	20.00
20.30*	21.00*
21.30	22.15

L2 LOS LLANOS DE ARIDANE - PUERTO DE TAZACORTE

Departures from

Los Llanos de Aridane	Puerto de Tazacorte
06.30*	07.00*
07.30*	08.00*
08.30	09.00
09.30	10.00
10.30	11.00
11.30	12.00
12.30	13.00
13.30	14.00
14.30	15.00
15.30	16.00
16.30	17.00
17.30	18.00
18.30	19.00
19.30	20.00
20.30	21.00

L3 SANTA CRUZ DE LA PALMA - LOS LLANOS DE ARIDANE via SAN JOSÉ, LEDAS, MAZO & FUENCALIENTE

For Los Llanos de Aridane
Departures from

S. C. de La Palma	Fuencaliente
06.00*	06.45*
08.00	08.45
10.00	10.45
12.00	12.45
13.15* (T) Terminates at Mazo	
14.15*	14.45*
16.00*	16.45*
18.15	18.45
20.15	20.45
21.45	

For Santa Cruz de La Palma
Departures from

Los Llanos de Aridane	Fuencaliente	Bus Station
06.00*	06.30*	06.45*
08.00	08.30	08.45
10.00	10.30	10.45
12.00*	12.30*	12.45*
14.00*	14.30*	14.45*
16.00*	16.30	16.45
18.00	18.30	18.45
20.00	20.30	20.45

L4 LOS LLANOS DE ARIDANE - PUERTO NAOS - CHARCO VERDE

Departures from

Los Llanos de Aridane	Puerto Naos	Charco Verde
06.30*	07.00*	06.50*
07.30*	08.00*	07.50*
08.30	09.00	08.50
09.00*	09.30*	09.20*
09.30	10.00	
10.00*	10.30*	10.20*
10.30	11.00	
11.00*	11.30*	11.20*
11.30	12.00	
12.00*	12.30*	12.20*
12.30	13.00	
13.00*	13.30*	13.20*
13.30	14.00	
14.00*	14.30*	14.20*
14.30	15.00	14.50
15.30	16.00	15.50
16.30	17.00	16.50
17.30	18.00	17.50
18.30	17.00	18.50
19.30	20.00	19.50
20.30	21.00	20.50

L5 LOS LLANOS DE ARIDANE - SANTO DOMINGO

Departures from

Los Llanos de Aridane	Santo Domingo
	05.30* (1)
06.30* (T)	06.00* (2)
07.15*	07.00* (1)
	07.30 (1)
	08.00* (2)
	09.00 (2)
10.30	11.00* (1)
12.30*	12.00* (2)
14.00*	14.30* (1)
	15.00* (2)
16.30* (3)	16.30 (1)
	17.15 (2)
19.30	

(1) via Garafía
(2) via Las Tricias
(3) via Gallegos

L7 SANTA CRUZ DE LA PALMA - TIGALATE via EL HOYO

Departures from

S. C. de La Palma	Tigalate
09.30*	07.00*
12.00*	10.00*
14.15*	12.30*
18.15*	15.00*
	17.00*

L8 SANTA CRUZ DE LA PALMA - CANCAJOS - AIRPORT

Departures from

S. C. de La Palma	Airport
	07.20* (3)
07.15	07.45*
07.45	08.15
08.15*	08.45*
08.45	09.15

					06.30*	06.50*	07.15*
06.00*	07.00*	07.30	07.50	08.15
		09.30*	09.50*	10.15*
		11.30	11.50	12.15
		13.30*	13.50*	14.15*
13.00*	14.00*	15.30	15.50	16.15
		17.30*	17.50*	18.15*
		19.30	19.50	20.15

09.15*	09.45*
09.45	10.15
10.15*	10.45*
10.45	11.15
11.15*	11.45*
11.45	12.15
12.15*	12.45*
12.45	13.15
13.15*	13.45*
13.45	14.15
14.15*	14.45*
14.45	15.15
15.15*	15.45*
15.45	16.15
16.15*	16.45*
16.45	17.15
17.15*	17.45*
17.45	18.15
18.45	19.15
19.45	20.15
20.45	21.15

(3) leaves from **Cancajos**

L14 SANTA CRUZ DE LA PALMA - SAN ISIDRO

Departures from

S. C de La Palma	San Isidro
08.45*	07.15*
10.45	09.30*
12.45*	11.30
14.15*	13.30*
16.45	15.30*
18.15*	17.30

L31 LOS CANARIOS - FARO via LAS INDIAS & CERCA VIEJA

Departures to **Faro** from

Canarios	Indias	Cerca Vieja
09.00	09.15	
11.00	11.15	11.30
15.00	15.15	15.30
17.00	17.15	
19.00	19.15	19.30

Departures to **Los Canarios** from

Faro	Cerca Vieja	Indias
10.00	10.15	
11.45	12.00	12.15
15.45	16.00	16.15
18.00	18.15	
19.45	20.00	20.15

* No Sunday or fiesta service
* No Saturday, Sunday or fiesta service

L11 SANTA CRUZ DE LA PALMA - PUNTALLANA - LOS SAUCES - BARLOVENTO - GALLEGOS- SANTO DOMINGO

Departures to the north, from

S. C. de La Palma	Punt-allana	Sauces	Barl-ovento	Gallegos
07.10	07.25	08.000	8.30*	09.00*
08.10*	08.25*	09.00*		
10.10	10.25	11.00		
12.10*	12.25*	13.00*		
14.10	14.25	15.00	15.30*	16.00*
16.10*	16.25*	17.00*		
18.10	18.25	19.00		
20.10*	20.25*	21.00*		
21.45	22.05	22.35		

Departures from the north to **Santa Cruz de La Palma**, from

Santo Domingo	Gallegos	Barl-ovento	Sauces	Punt-allana
		05.00	05.20	05.45

Bus lines and waymarked paths that cross them

Ask in the Tourist Information Office for up-to-date detailed timetables.

Line N°
L1	GR130, PRs1, 13.3, & 14
L2	GR130, GR131, PR1
L3	GR130, GR131, PRs 14.1, 15, 16, 17, & 18
L4	GR130, PR1
L5	GR130, GR131, PRs 10, 11, & 12, SLs 51, 55, 62, & 71
L7	GR130, PRs 15, 16, 17, & 18
L8	PR18
L11	GR130, PRs 3, 4, 5, 6, 7, 8, 9, & 10, SLs 21, 40, 51

La Palma

Tour & Trail

1:40,000 Scale Map

Super-Durable Edition
Waterproof & Super-Tou

Fully Updated 2005 Edi
on Super-Durable polyr
£7.99 UK / €11.50 La Palm

Discovery Walking Guides Ltd
ISBN 1-904946-07-0
Copyright David & Ros Brawn

HOW TO GET HOLD OF OUR PUBLICATIONS

Ask in any bookshop, order from amazon.co.uk, via our websites, or order direct from us by mail order, using the form below.

If you are ordering direct from us, please:

- complete your details in BLOCK CAPITALS
- write the full title(s) of the publications you require
- enclose your payment (please note that post & packing is free)
- make your cheque payable to:

Discovery Walking Guides Ltd.
and post to:
Discovery Walking Guides Ltd.
10 Tennyson Close
Northampton NN5 7HJ

TITLE(S) ORDERED	ITEM COST

I enclose my cheque for this **TOTAL**
(free post & packing)

YOUR NAME	
ADDRESS	
POST CODE	
*TEL N°	
**email	@

* for order enquiries only   ** for enewsletters and updates

DISCOVERY WALKING GUIDES LTD. TITLES LIST

GPS NAVIGATION

GPS The Easy Way
Manual £4.99
PERSONAL NAVIGATOR FILES
Version 2.01 Downloadable GPS
records for all Walk!/Walks Guidebooks +
GPS Utility Software
CD £7.99

SPANISH MAINLAND

Sierra de Aracena - a Walk! Guidebook
Guidebook £11.99
Sierra de Aracena
Tour & Trail Map £2.99
34 Alpujarras Walks
Guidebook £9.99
Alpujarras Super-Durable
Tour & Trail Map £7.99
Walk! Axarquia
Guidebook £11.99

CANARY ISLANDS

Walk! Lanzarote
Guidebook £11.99
Lanzarote Super-Durable
Tour & Trail Map £7.99
Lanzarote Indestructible Map £4.99

Lanzarote Plant&Flower Guide £2

Walk! La Gomera (2nd edition)
Guidebook £11.99
La Gomera Super-Durable
Tour & Trail Map £7.99
Drive! La Gomera
Touring Map £2.50

35 Tenerife Walks
Guidebook £9.99
Tenerife Super-Durable
Walkers' Maps £4.99
Tenerife Paper Edition
Walkers' Maps £2.99
Tenerife Indestructible Map £4.99

Drive! Tenerife Touring Map £2.50

Tenerife Plant&Flower Guide £2

Gran Canaria Mountains
Tour & Trail Map £5
Gran Canaria Plant&Flower Guide £2

Walk! La Palma
Guidebook £11.99
La Palma Super-Durable
Tour & Trail Map £7.99

BALEARIC ISLANDS

Walk! Mallorca (North & Mountains)
Guidebook £11.99
Mallorca North & Mountains Super-Durable
Tour & Trail Map £7.99
Walk! Mallorca West
Guidebook £11.99

Walk! Menorca
Guidebook £11.99
Menorca Super-Durable
Tour & Trail Map £7.99
Drive! Menorca
Touring Map £2.50

ANDORRA

Walk! Andorra
Guidebook £11.99

PORTUGAL, INCLUDING MADEIRA

Madeira Super-Durable
Tour & Trail Map £7.99
35 Madeira Walks
Guidebook £9.99
Drive! Madeira
Touring Map £2.50

Algarve - Loule
Walking Guide £5
Algarve - Silves
Walking Guide £5

MALTA & GOZO

Malta & Gozo Walking Guides £5